When God Says NO!

A Celebration of Adversity

When God Says NO!: A Celebration of Adversity
Copyright © 2023 by Benjamin F. Simmons Jr.

Published in the United States of America
ISBN   Paperback: 979-8-89091-306-7
ISBN   eBook: 979-8-89091-307-4

All rights reserved. No part of this publication may be reproduced, stored in a retrieval system or transmitted in any way by any means, electronic, mechanical, photocopy, recording or otherwise without the prior permission of the author except as provided by USA copyright law.

The opinions expressed by the author are not necessarily those of ReadersMagnet, LLC.

ReadersMagnet, LLC
10620 Treena Street, Suite 230 | San Diego, California, 92131 USA
1.619. 354. 2643 | www.readersmagnet.com

Book design copyright © 2023 by ReadersMagnet, LLC. All rights reserved.

Cover design by Tifanny Curaza
Interior design by Dorothy Lee

When God Says NO!

A Celebration of Adversity

DECEMBER 10, 2022
AUTHOR: BENJAMIN F SIMMONS JR
2716 Arlington Drive APT 201 Alexandria VA 22306

ReadersMagnet, LLC

TABLE OF CONTENTS

Preface vii
Introduction ix

Chapter 1 His Word, His Will, and His Way 1
    The Word of God 3
    The Will of God 6
    The Way of God 8
Chapter 2 Adversity - Friend or Foe? 11
Chapter 3 Born of a Woman 14
    The pursuit of economic stabilization 17
    Making It work thru a continuum of challenges 18
Chapter 4 The Anatomy of Storm 20
Chapter 5 A Time to Pray 26
Chapter 6 Walking on Water 33
Chapter 7 Take Off Thy Shoes 39
Chapter 8 The Challenge of Faith 44
Chapter 9 A Plumb Line for My Faith 54
Chapter 10 What is That Good? Roman 12:2 79
Chapter 11 A True Story of Adversity 87

PREFACE

The mystery of Gods Will and Way are deliberately reserved for revelation in time and season by His choosing alone. The subject of this journey necessarily considers a hypothetical case study for human suffering with a supporting thesis. No one is exempt from suffering throughout life. Unfortunately, biblical discourse remains completely void of plausible apologetics for adversity. Contrary to academic resolve, man does not have the intellectual capacity to gauge or comprehend the perfect Will of God. Neither can the divine objectives of God for one's life be reverse engineered from biblical accounts.

The glory and divine assignments of God also remains void of duplication. What was for Peter, was not for Paul. It is however safe to claim that the Will of God is good for all without appeal. Nevertheless, you may ponder why the Goodness and Power of God permits suffering from cradle to grave? Suffering appears to play a systemic role in the human experience. You are not alone. After you complete this literary investigation, you will at least know that an undisclosed good follows each storm of life.

Theological consensus may implicate five (5) biblical culprits for suffering to include: the imputed sin of a predecessor, a self-inflicted hardship due to unhealthy or ill advice risks, Gods punitive response to individual sin, Demonic powers, or the works of God for a greater glory. It is the latter that predisposes the narrative of this book. Better grab a handkerchief, this journey collides adversity and a symphony of broken hearts.

INTRODUCTION

A certain man was known for his wisdom. He carefully planned for all the current and future needs of his family with clinical detail. He then found the perfect plot of land and designed/built a home that would accommodate his family to include growth, sustenance, safety, recreation, faith, education, storm, fire, hail, scenery, access to medical services and all the requisite needs of his family. There would be no need for any further development for the life of his home, lest it implicate an oversight of the wise man during the initial design phase. So, it is with our God.

He knows the end from the beginning and designs all his creation for an undisclosed purpose. The hypothesis of this biblical investigation asserts adversity as a mission of divine glory as opposed to human character development. God is not making you a better person when you suffer adversity. Your strengths and your weaknesses all work together for good, and your gifts and talents have already been

DNA installed. Nevertheless, there is always at least one beneficiary blessed by your suffering.

This book is for faith that died, tears that cried, and prayers placed on mute by the finger of God. Perhaps you have considered filing a *false claim lawsuit* against the promise of prayer and throw in the towel on a hope *"that maketh not ashamed" Roman 5:5*. Your bad news graduated to worse, and your worst-case outcome has left you in a faithless conundrum. Perhaps you feel you have breached the law of God or have not been good enough to merit His favor. Is my hope in vain? When you feel this way, you are never alone.

Can we talk? You will necessarily suffer between conception and interment with sparse apologetics. No one is exempt from the diagnosis of adversity. As humans we have an innate predispose to reason why, but what does one do when reason and console have not been appropriated? Surely God is good and more than able to preclude, heal and/or restore. However, what are we missing when prayer seems void of answer? Yes ... sometimes our Heavenly Father's answer is NO! When our heavenly father says no, a far greater interests is underway. Be of good cheer!

Perhaps Gods denial of a prayer request convict's dilemma as culprit of a greater glory. One that necessarily falls within His permissive will. Recall in biblical history many innocent unblemished male lambs were slain for the atonement of human sin. When they themselves had done no wrong. What if someone other than yourself is the beneficiary of your suffering? If you are currently standing in the wake or on the shore of adversity, welcome to resolve. We will take a clinical look at several biblical case studies that lay the foundation for a response to the greatest theological question concerning adversity, better known as "Why?".

CHAPTER 1

His Word, His Will, and His Way

I think it meet to begin our journey with a clarification and working knowledge of how we reference and view the intent and directives of our God for His creation. This is not an easy task because there are as many different theological perspectives as there are people on the planet. Permit me to assert if you will. We are All in need of theological disabuse. Yes. Even I stand as chief among the uncertain. You see, the most revered Apostle Paul was both an accomplished Jewish Official and a drum major for the spread of Christianity like none other, yet he also conceded uncertainty concerning the theodicy of God. His commitment to the spread of the Gospel of Christ earned him frequent incarcerations, physical abuse, life threats, and ultimately martyrdom.

The apostle Paul was no stranger to adversity. Later we will take a closer look at his experiences in detail. Paul necessarily admits in the first epistle he wrote to the Church at Corinth, that his understanding of God is like seeing through a dark glass 1 Corinthian 13:12. By this statement he essentially admits that a perfect theology will only manifest when we see God face to face as he further asserts, "only then will I know Him as I am known" [1 Corinthian 13:12]. God does not provide detailed enumerations for why we must suffer even while doing good works. It is a mystery void of reason, nevertheless sufficed for a season by faith alone.

God knows us beyond our comprehension as He is our creator, but He robes Himself with a cloud of mystery. We cannot look upon Him or see His face in our human form for reasons unknown and unsearchable. Seeing Him is an experience necessarily reserved for a time and season beyond the human experience. How then can we know his Word, His Way, or His Will and what do these references even imply? Who shall claim they have the knowledge of God? All is by faith with two exceptions. He will on occasion speak within our hearing with a still small voice and/or show us, His Hand. The plan of God is not easily discerned from theological academics. The sacred biblical accounts afford a praiseworthy glimpse of His glory, but the mystery of God is appropriated by His choosing alone.

Man can only gather, review, and assess the ancient scriptures (e. g. biblical accounts) more commonly known as testaments of God. Such were harvested from the archives of time and canonized by review, integration, and assimilation into what we all know as the bible. It is from this source that one may meticulously ascertain the mission, goals, and objectives of an unseen God. A God who at various and sundry times speaks to some, seen of none, and displays His power before many. Herein lies the predicate for the global division and the manifestation of a broad range of belief systems all promulgated by persuasion as the authentic God given directives for life and the requisite values for an eternal reward in heaven. Fasten your seat belt. We are about to fly through some turbulent theological precepts.

The Word of God

The "Word of God" is an expression that is frequently used as a code reference to the Bible as we know it today. References to the "Word of God" may also be used to imply God given moral directives for man to abide. It is easy to identify a plethora of biblical passages that represent good moral behavior for all to abide. However, it may be a tad presumptuous to glean God's plan and directives for any one individual as a product of biblical context. The moral directives detailed in the holy scriptures necessarily apply to all. The Bible commemorates a chronicle of prophetic experiences and interactions with God dating back thousands of years.

Each Prophet was anointed of God for a specific assignment and none of the prophets assumed the call of another. Each prophet experienced an intimate and direct line of communication with God concerning their divine missions, goals, and objectives. In addition to the scriptural "Word of God ", there is also the "Audible Voice of God" reserved only by divine choosing of His elect. Such is the sacred and undisputed "Word of God". This rare "audible voice" experience is not gleaned from scriptural etymology, context, and culture assimilated by theological scholars. Such an experience is Holy and accompanied by the indescribable power of His presence. Only Moses could go to the top of Mount Sinai.

Please do not feel deficient or deprived if you have matriculated a PHD in Religion and a Doctoral

Degree in theology and have never heard the audible voice of God. God does not speak audibly to everyone. This does not mean you have an unsubstantiated role in His will. It simply denotes your assignment does not require audible inform. Always remember, every grain of sand on the beach has an assignment but not all are touched by the oscillating tide. In the next segment we will necessarily investigate the reference to Gods Will. It is important to note that the "Word of God" is always Holy, Direct, and Intimate, but sparsely Corporate. A contemporary biblical orator may craft inspiring messages, but they are necessarily engineered for corporate consumption.

In summary, we must understand and make an honorable distinction between the written, spoken, and living "Word of God". The written word may be best revered as the canonization of documented human experiences with God often referenced as scriptures. The spoken "Word of God" is a rare one on one experience where a man receives the audible instruct of God always in a private setting. Finally, we have the living word as recorded in the gospel according to John 1:14 "and the word was made flesh and dwelt among us". Jesus himself has been identified by scripture as the living Word and everything he spoke was suitable for instruction to the hearer.

The Will of God

To begin our assessment of the Will of God for our lives, perhaps we should start with a working definition of what a will represents using a secular example. We are all familiar with a last Will and Testament which is prepared by a person to instruct legal authorities regarding how to disperse assets and financial holdings to heirs in the event of the demise of same. By this popular example we can safely assert the will of an individual as a plan of action for designated recipients undisclosed and ineffective until a designated time. Such a plan may include specific equities for each heir as well as common appropriations for all heirs. Finally, it is important to note that once a Will has been codified it cannot be altered by the behavior of the recipient/s because *a Will is not a performance-based product*.

Before we go deeper into turbulent theological waters it is essential to define an engineering concept called *reverse engineering*. This term is used to represent an engineering exercise performed to derive a completely unknown entity from trace elements using inference. This engineering *modus operandi* is a precise caricature of any attempt to derive the Will of God for your life from biblical accounts and testimonies.

The bible is a collection of human experiences with the divine glory of God written and translated time and again over thousands of years. Although the Bible contains a clear indictment against human immorality, God alone in His own time and means will specify the unique calling upon your life. The Will of God is a deliberate orchestration of time and events for both corporate and individual concerns all working together for an undiscernible objective called *good*.

Contrary to popular performance-based theology, God is not incarcerated by the sin nature and disobedience of man. His Will has factored in human disobedience and His objectives are on course for a timely, successful, and intentional completion for everyone and all collectively. Please also be advised that the Will of God is not transactional as some may assert. There are no cases where God cannot do "B" until man does "A". The Will of God cannot be altered or impeded by human behavior. He knows the end from the beginning, and He Is the author and finisher of our faith. God is never victim of human circumstance.

The Way of God

It is written that God's ways are not our ways, and His thoughts are not like our thoughts [Isaiah 55:8]. God made time in the crucible of His hand to serve His Will and bow down at His throne. God can press pause, and time will stand still, and no one would know or detect His universal stay of execution. His knowledge is unsearchable and beyond decipher by human intellect. He is Alpha and Omega, so His way is not pending outcome to proceed. The product of His hand is perfect with no need for quality assurance protocol. He can orchestrate human events over time to render the product of His Will with a way void of disclose. The very notion of the Apostle Paul statement that "all things work together for good" [Romans 8:28] implicates God's orchestrated power. Having all power, God neither "wants" or 'tries' anything as men do void of the knowledge of outcome.

Perhaps the most difficult concept to embrace concerning the way of God is understanding how His permissive Will and Way incorporates adversity to effectuate a greater good. Adversity seems to be better applied as a punitive response to human disobedience, but the record shows that is not the Way of God. His punitive response to the sin of man He placed upon himself and nailed it to a Cross. Think of how many times you have done that for your enemy. Excuse me, I need to pause right here to address these tears. Okay, since He himself has paid for our sin, we should never view adversity as the wrath of God against the sin of man, but rather something more systemic and orchestrated within the Way of God.

Contrary to popular theology we cannot always pray away adversity as it plays a systemic role in the Way of God. Regretfully, this also means that some people you pray for may not survive their illness or accidental calamity. This is not good news *prima facia* and is never celebrated in the pulpit or as a function of standard theology. We must conclude that no man can matriculate expert status on the Word, the Will, or the Way of God which is why we have the mandate of Faith. We must also conclude that the Way of God is not transactional pending prerequisites of human behavior.

How then should man read the bible? As a performance directive? As a testimony of Faith? As the mystery of God? As a moral mandate? As requisite requirement for a heavenly reward? The answer is all the above with caution. Many biblical accounts enumerate directives that were targeted exclusively for the prophets. Be sure to distinguish between a directive to "Love thy Neighbor as thyself" and "Go tell Pharaoh to let my people go". Not all biblical scriptures should be construed as executable directives for all men to abide but rather for moral inform. Sorry but there can be no experts on the Word, the Will, or the Way of God. Let us therefore be content with the following:

The **Will** of God is Good. The **Word** of God is Sure. However, the **Way** of God consistently eludes discernment.

CHAPTER 2

Adversity - Friend or Foe?

Life is filled with adversity from birth to eternal commencement. How we view and define adversity will play a major role in how we perceive the human experience and the Way of God. The classic definition offered in most dictionaries describes adversity as any calamity, disaster, misfortune, or troubled state of affair. Such a definition implies egregious suffering which leaves nothing to appreciate, celebrate or look forward to. According to the Gospel of Peter a key follower of Christ he shares in 1st Peter 4:12-13 "Beloved, think it not strange concerning the fiery trial which is to try you … But rejoice, in as much as ye are partakers of Christ's sufferings". Peter further deliberates the fruit of adversity in 1st Peter 5:10 by sharing "after that ye have suffered a while God will restore, establish, strengthen, and settle you".

Now we have a classic biblical conundrum to decipher. Peter clearly asserts sufferings as both deliberate and essential to the human experience. If adversity serves a greater good and is clearly appropriated by the Will of God for such, how does one negotiate its celebration? In the Garden of Gethsemane Jesus attempts to pray away the egregious suffering of His pending crucifixion but after great deliberation He concedes that His agony would serve a greater good. Could it be when God says No to our prayer requests that a greater good is underway?

The bible is also fraught with prayer and supplication bringing forth miraculous healings and recovery from diverse maladies, misfortunes, and hardships. Now we have classified two types of adversity with distinctly different missions. The latter healing of the sick by prayer illuminates and glorifies the power of God to deliver man from the bondage of affliction. The former reference to adversity in the Garden of gethsemane suggests God has also a suffering that bares divine assignment. How then shall prayer profit with the veil of uncertainty? Did not the wind and waves obey when the Lord said, "Peace be still"?

What then shall we draw from the proverbial well of conclusions? We are necessarily on a collision course with trial and tribulation from birth to promotion. Adversity is a classroom with Anguish serving as a Schoolmaster. As soon as one storm has passed for a season a new cloud begins to darken the sky. It seems we go through a vicious cycle from storm to tornado with no end in sight. But be of good cheer! He has overcome the world and paved the way for our promotion to glory. It does not yet appear what we shall be (1 John 3:2). Above the Dark clouds and Strong winds, the Sun shines still. Our Creator and heavenly Father is precisely on course to achieve an expected end. He is the only wise God without fail!

CHAPTER 3

Born of a Woman

Adversity/tribulation makes its debut at birth in the form of labor pains. Life commences with a struggle through a tight canal and suddenly you arrive in a place contaminated with bright light as cold as a winters chill. You are completely naked in a delivery room when the Doctor has the audacity to strike you as if you had done something wrong. Thanks for the blanket, but what was the assault all about? By the way, who is the lady in the bed who keeps staring at me? Is she going to hit me too? Please note how suffering has an undisclosed mission even from the beginning. Thank God our first tears are short lived and immediately followed by the embrace and cuddle appropriated solely by a mothers' arms.

Welcome to the journey of life commencing with struggle and calamity becomes the norm. In the book of Job, he shares that life is fraught with distress, seemingly by design "man is born of a woman a few days full of trouble" Job 14:1. The important thing to underscore and appreciate is the deliberate nature of our struggles. Something systemic is taking place to render an end-product in each case. Each struggle in life has the same recipe which includes a dash of distress, a touch of anxiety, a sprinkle of tears with an occasional side of broken heart.

Can we take a stroll down memory lane? It may be a tad foggy to remember the difficulty we experienced learning to walk and navigate a spoon without making a mess for someone else to clean up. Cutting teeth was no picknick either but the pain is now vague and all but erased from memory. Then came learning to walk, falling, and trying again until we got it right. All incredibly unique struggles of life now deep in the archives of our memory. In fact, it was that bicycle fall and bruised knee that hurt like h*ll that became a successful balance Instructor. As we gaze into the review mirror of life, adversity seems to have always yielded a product from the very beginning.

If you thought learning to walk, eat, ride a bike, and share your stuff with your siblings was a challenge, then you faced a 16-year academic development mandate before entering the workforce. Not to mention a crescendo of biological interests and desires for an invisible force called "cute" that never failed to eclipse the academic focus. A 16-year stint of non-negotiable intellectual development ensues that was curious and a tad uncomfortable at best. What on earth am I going to be when all this academic developmental stuff is done? No one really has and answer for what career path and title awaits you following commencement but whatever it will be it must be worth the journey.

Clearly life proves to be a continuum of challenging experiences for some future need for oneself and for the help and assistance of others. Each phase of life proves to have discomforts, obstacles, disappointments, and calamity ultimately leading to a greater good for all. At times, our experiences can be so frustrating we feel victimized and defeated by circumstance which causes us to seek a higher power and authority for consolation and resolve. Yes, tribulation will put us on our knees. Grandma sang an unforgettable verse of an old country church song a long, long time ago. She sang a song entitled "you'll understand it better by and by". What a true revelation of the human experience.

So, you complete your academic tour with great travail. You have a friend who seems to be that special one and now you need a job. You find yourself reading the want ads for employment opportunities where the requisite experience seems far more suitable for someone other than yourself. Your one-page resume shows educational achievement, but your experience is anemic at best. The experience you matriculated at the Pizza Place and the Grocery Store is not match for your career objectives. Now you face the proof of qualification. Yet another testimony of life's continuum of trial and tribulation. A subtle implication that challenge is a never-ending norm working behind the scenes of life.

The pursuit of economic stabilization

Time moves on and you marry the love of your life and with exception of infrequent spats, things are going well. First baby is on the way, and you are trying to figure out if you can afford a larger place or just make do with the one-bedroom apartment for now. If your pending promotion comes through it will give you just the income you need to make ends meet. Nothing seems promising and the air is full of both hope and uncertainty. The coveted stable personal economy versus the paycheck-to-paycheck modus operandi seems to dominate this phase of life. Together you decide to join the local church to meet new friends and receive a much-needed inspiration for your family growth challenges. It never occurs that something orchestrated by the hand of God is underway.

Making It work thru a continuum of challenges

Time eludes you once again and you wake up with three teenage kids and a receding hair line. The Doctor has detected your slightly elevated blood pressure and has you on a daily medication to keep things under control. One child is ready for college but not sure what she really wants to select as a major. Another is predisposed with music, guitars, pop bands and the latest fashion of clothes. The baby is thirteen and obsessed with video games and does not have a clue what comes next after middle school. Faith and love seem to be the anchor that stabilizes the proverbial ship and endures one storm after the other.

Wife has joined the church choir and those frequent spats have decreased to a peaceful and loving coexistence cultivated by more frequent acknowledgements of the goodness of God. Family challenges have birthed a growing frequency in the demand for faith. A faith formerly perceived solely for religious people now takes a curious residency in your home. Maybe there is a God which knows all about our trouble and appropriates resolve accordingly. Maybe the storms of life play a systemic role in the glory of God and his will for our lives. Oh well, better get the groceries and gas for the car for now.

CHAPTER 4

The Anatomy of Storm

Perhaps it's best to establish a working definition of the proverbial "Storm" before we use it metaphorically to define the nature and response to an adversarial experience. Understanding the anatomy of adversity also segues the next chapter which necessarily examines the impetus and response to our experience. A classic storm may be described as strong force winds often accompanied by heavy precipitation (e. g. rain, snow, sleet, hail) capable of uprooting structures and carrying airborne satellites destroying or severely damaging everything in its path. Please note that the fundamental notion of a storm is both disruptive, damaging and/or destructive. This definition becomes the basis for why we frequently reference adversity as a storm of life.

Every Storm we experience essentially consists of three phases to include: (1) anticipation or prelude to chaos, (2) the manifestation and confirmation of a bad condition, and (3) acceptance, navigation and recovery from collateral damages. Each phase of a storm warrants careful appraisal to articulate a responsive prayer that complements uncertainty and anxiety. Understanding the anatomy of our trials and tribulations helps us to both navigate the turbulent waters and anchor our faith in God until the storm has passed. Please also note that it is never easy to think with such strategic eloquence during a storm. This book affords the opportunity to take a rational look at devastating experiences to affectively negotiate a true storm before the sky darkens. Always remember, emotion will be the loudest voice in the wheelhouse of your dilemma.

> **Phase 1** of the Storm is the period where the sky darkens with disheartening news. You brace your heart for what could become a catastrophic inform, while hoping for the best. Faith somehow moves to the back seat while secular resolve is now in charge of the steering wheel. What on earth are we

going to do now? The doctors report tells a grim story. Time is of essence, and you feel somewhat overwhelmed with what could happen. Strange how quickly our church going, choir singing, hand clapping, seed sowing amends have become noisy ceremony. The gray sky of bad news has eclipsed the glory of God with a thick layer of doom and gloom which fills the room. Then someone has the audacity to say, "don't worry, God will make a way". Please allow me a minute here before I continue. This grim occasion is for too familiar.

Phase 2 of the Storm commences when your worst nightmare is now confirmed. The Doctors X-ray, CAT Scan, and Ultrasound test results confirm in concert that it's time to call all family members and prepare for the worst. You will never forget the moment the Doctor walks in with that hopeless look on his face to share a heartfelt sentiment "we did all we could". This is the apex of your challenge that demands either the concession of defeat or a greater faith through the storm like a mighty warrior. The battle between your faith, hope, prayers, and outcome are now on trial in the courtroom of your heart. Surely God heard your prayer and the prayers of others for same. Now you must continue to pray and hope against hope believing for a miracle while a loved one is transferred to hospice care. Surely God is able.

Phase 3 of the storm commences when the phone rings and a still small voice announces that a loved one has passed. The hospice care provider immediately request that you arrange to remove the body within a short period of time. No time for weeping and wailing although that's all you feel on the inside. You must gather insurance policies and select a funeral home to immediately schedule a removal of the body from the care facility. Phase 3 of the adversity model is best known for the period where we must re-evaluate the purpose of prayer in our lives. You prayed for your situation when it was diagnosed and instead of improvement or resolve it got worse. This is not what you were preached on Sunday morning. You were told if you ask in "His Name" and believed in your heart you would receive that which you have asked. The stage is now set to necessarily re-assess your faith and the validity of the claim of prayer.

Now that we have covered the three (3) phases of adversity A.K.A. the Storm, it is important to note that a health-related crisis was only used as an example to model a devastating experience. Adversity may manifest in a panoply of states of imperil. It is also Important to note that the severity of a storm is governed by perception and emotional bonds to the one/s who are suffering. Perception and faith will determine whether you see an undefeated Giant or an "Uncircumcised Philistine" 1 Samuel 17:26 metaphorically speaking. Such was the case concerning the story of David and Goliath in the bible. This biblical case study simply challenges one to assess whether they are viewing adversity through the lens of victory or defeat. It is also paramount to note that winning the war may mean losing some of the battles. Be sure to install an optimistic perspective for each storm. Things may get worse before they get better.

In the crucible of optimism, there are two key biblical charisms including faith and hope. The fragility of a trust in God is exposed when faith and hope both become frustrated. An impotent faith will manifest when the answer to your prayer does not appear eminent. It is not unusual in such cases to question the integrity of what you were taught concerning a faith that "moves mountains" and the "fervent and effectual prayer of the righteous". Faith, Hope and Prayer are inextricably connected. Each of these biblical mandates must be complemented with patience and cradled in the arms of time. Unfortunately, your faith embodies your belief system, while your hope relentlessly negotiates possibility. Faith must become the predicate for hope as hope facilitates the fervent and effectual prayer. If you don't receive what you have prayed for something far greater must be at work. In the next chapter we necessarily cover the impetus, content, hope, and product of prayer.

CHAPTER 5

A Time to Pray

What shall we ask of a God concerning our circumstance? A God who is omniscient, omnipresent, omnipotent and loves us more than we can fathom. Omniscient means He has all knowledge which renders prayer void of inform. Omnipresence means He is in all places at the same time and in all times at the same place of authority. Omnipotent means he has all power in His hand to preclude, restore, resolve, or permit pursuant His Will. There is no need for an eloquent exposition of the prognosis, diagnosis, or bleak outlook of circumstance. He knows the end from the beginning of all things. He made tear ducts for crying and hearts to be broken and mended by His love. He knows all about a bed fraught with toss and turn and a pillow that refuses the quest for sleep. What then shall I ask of God when my knees have given my feet a rest?

Perhaps the greatest description of our relationship with God is embodied by the notion of a Heavenly Father. Our earthly father/parents facilitated all our needs from birth until we matriculated our first job. Even then we had to call home from time to time for advice, guidance, and yes even a little extra cash when resource fell short of debt and obligation. We are well acquainted with the notion of father and the supplication for the things which we need or desire. Jesus taught his disciples to pray using the parental model in the classic Lord's Prayer. Jesus later shared with his disciples that your heavenly father already knows what you have need of before you ask. [Matthew 6:32]

An interesting theological question concerning prayer was entertained many years ago. Can a human prayer request alter or refine the plan or will of God? If your answer is no, then you may agree with John Calvin a 16th century Christian recognized as the progenitor of the notion that all things are predestined (Calvinism) by God and cannot be altered. The story is told that St. Augustine a Catholic icon and Martin Luther the founder of the Protestant reformation both agreed that God could not be manipulated as John

Calvin asserted in his predestination thesis. This was a profound instance of agreement between radically different perceptions of God's will for His creation.

What we know as Calvinism today embodies the notion that the will of God is necessarily preordained and cannot be altered. The audacity of Calvinism is perhaps the very reason why God already knows what you have need of before you ask Mathew 6:8. However, opposing arguments of the human experience also raise an interesting question concerning the biblical mandate for godly behavior which yields eternal reward or punishment. Can free will be uniformly integrated into a preordained outcome for humanity? The short answer is yes, but let's dig a little deeper.

In the study of algebra, a precursor of higher collegiate academics we are introduced to the notion of a variable. A complex algebraic expression may contain one or more variables and constants to produce a range of outcomes as the embedded variables assume different values. The mission and objective of the overarching equation are not altered by the variables contained within its framework. As it is with equations and complex mathematic formulas with embedded variables, the Will of God is not altered or impeded by constituent human dynamics. Oh, how excellent is our God! His knowledge is unsearchable.

The bible is fraught with prayer requests from genesis to revelations, however not all prayer petitions were complemented by divine resolve as hoped. Why did not all prayer requests receive an in-kind response? Understanding the divine will of God means each prayer request may be appropriated as articulated or declined for a greater objective. If you are expecting to receive the same outcome for your prayer as recorded for other biblical characters you may be in route to disappointment. When God says no a greater work is always underway. The anguish permitted by an unanswered prayer facilitates divine assignment for a higher call within God's will. It is written in Luke 12:48 ".. to whom much is given much is also required ..". We have a biblical mandate to "Be of good cheer" John 16:33, even if we must provide temporary housing for a broken heart.

The product of prayer is best spoken of by James 5:16 *"The fervent and effectual prayer of the righteous avails much"* which does not exact outcome but assures a product of great value if the prayer qualifies as stated. It is also important to note that this scriptural reference does not implicate a response time for the answer to prayer. No biblical expository is provided for how long one must wait for the answer of prayer. The author of this verse found in the book of James

5:16 necessarily relegates response time to the will of God. In the book of Job, he is recorded as saying he would "Wait till my change come" Job 14:14 which is completely void of a specific time constraint. By now you may be thinking, what about people who do not solely rely upon prayers but have the anointed power to effectuate change.

There is a strange dichotomy between healing by anointed power and the healing afforded by the classic fervent and effectual prayer. Many believed they could be healed by the anointed shadow of Peter as recorded in Acts 5:15-16. A certain woman was also healed by simply touching the anointed hem of our Lords garment in a crowd. [Mathew 9:20] The term anoint has a variety of references in the bible. In general, it means to choose or to empower with divine power for a specific assignment from God. The term anoint may also reference a religious ceremonial procedure of the poring of oils on a person chosen for a Godly assignment. Nevertheless, whether one is anointed or simply a lay person petitioning God's help through prayer the healing remains within the will of God.

What then shall we ask of God when our knees have given our feet a rest? Before we begin our prayer, we must remind ourselves that God already knows the circumstance and situational detail far better than we can articulate. Prayer typically falls within three (3) functional areas including (1) Expressions of gratitude for what God has already done, (2) Supplications for resolve of a dilemma beyond human capacity, and/or (3) endurance thru an existing hardship. Please remain mindful and appreciate that prayer requests falling in category (2) as listed above are limited. In some cases, God says no to supplications that solicit exemption from hardship that are essential to a greater systemic calling. Your suffering may in fact play a major role in the deliverance of others. Allow me to reiterate that God is not making you a better person through adversity. Strength and Weakness are both by design. Sampson was strong by design.

The classic case where God's answer is no to a supplication is recorded in the New Testament Matthew 26:39 [… Oh My Father, if it is possible, let this cup pass from me…] this Jesus prayed in the garden of Gethsemane to exempt the need for him to suffer and die an egregious death on the cross and the answer from God was No. It is also important to note that there is no entitlement by righteous behavior to receive a prayer request. Jesus had no sin. In the case with Jesus, his death would play a systemic role in making salvation available to the entire world. So, it is in each of our lives when God says no something far greater is at work. When you pray for healing, recovery, deliverance, strength, patience, etc. always conclude with "if it be thy will". The book of Ecclesiastes is noted for the claim that there is a time and season for all things. Time and season cannot be altered by the prayer of men lest God issues a divine exemption of same.

CHAPTER 6

Walking on Water

In this chapter we necessarily reiterate the paramount need to navigate adversity with a carefully crafted and implemented perspective. How you perceive circumstance will inform your faith, hope, and endurance thru the storm. An unhealthy predispose with conditions could imperil a faith that moves mountains, defeats giants, and parts red seas. This is virtually impossible after the storm has overtaken you by surprise and all your efforts are expended managing your emotional response to bad news as it matriculates worst case scenario. Caution! A faithless perspective immediately cites statistical outcomes for similar adversities and concludes same for the existing circumstance. An army that perceives the enemy as a superior force will lay down their weapons, forfeit battle, and surrender without a fight. The bible states in Proverbs 23:7 *"as a man thinketh so is he"*.

How then shall we install a failsafe perspective for the storms of life? The first step in the process is to force the probability and statistics twins to be seated in the back seat completely void of opinion, perspective and/or recommendation, while Faith seats itself securely in the wheel house of the storm. Faith is the divine supplement for a mission solely housed in the bosom of God. A faith-based perception plays a critical role in establishing a resilient perspective through difficult times. But beware of reason who will make faith sound foolish. It is easy to reflect on previous outcomes for similar conditions and subsequently adopt a bleak outlook for your current dilemma. Perception may be informed by, optimism, pessimism, or a faith that rises above circumstance.

A clever writer once shared that "Pessimism asserts the glass is half empty while Optimism claims the glass is half full". However, an unwavering Faith is best illustrated in Habakkuk 3:17-19 "if the fig tree wont blossom and there is no fruit in the vine, labor of the olive shall fail and the field yields no meat, flock separated from the fold and no herd in the stall. Yet will I glory in the God of my salvation". In this scriptural passage the Biblical character Habakkuk prescribes the best perspective through adversity. No matter what his circumstance dictates or what outcome manifests there by Habakkuk's faith in God is rooted, grounded and immovable. Are you there yet?

In the referenced scripture above the biblical character named Habakkuk eloquently exposes his perspective thru adversity as never being contingent upon outlook, circumstance, or outcome. Neither is he moved by worst case scenario and the resulting possibilities. The only reason he can matriculate a graduate level thesis concerning adversity is because of his understanding and relationship with an all knowing and all-powerful God. Habakkuk was fully persuaded that if he does not receive what he prays and hopes for God is still able to sustain him through adversity and restore, recover, revive, and recreate from collateral damages. Habakkuk must have checked God's Balance Statement and found no debt, no foreclosures, no liens, no liabilities, and no losses. No losses? Don't make me shout by myself because I will. If God has no losses, where on earth did you acquire yours?

Perhaps Habakkuk was also well acquainted with the book of Joel that expounds how God is able to restore what "the locust, the canker worm, the Caterpillar, and the Palmer Worm has eaten" Joel

2:25. Maybe he was also familiar with the experience of Ezekiel in the valley of dry bones where God restores life to the dried bones of an army of deceased soldiers in Ezekiel 37:5 "… I will cause breath to enter into you. And ye shall live." God's restorative power is an essential focal point thru the storm when collateral damage seems eminent. Although extremely difficult, It is more than fruitful to think on these things in the worst of times to obtain a greater faith.

Perspective is the interrelation in which a subject and/or its parts are mentally viewed. Perspective is indicted, arrested, and convicted by focus. Unfortunately, focus is easily distracted by possibility and difficult at best to anchor when tried. To best illustrate the danger and volatility of a perspective distracted by focus, consider the story told in the book of Mathew 14:22-33 after ministering to over five (5) thousand in a desert place Jesus fed them with five (5) loaves of bread and two (2) small fishes. Jesus then sends his disciples to the other side of the Sea of Galilee by boat while he retreats for prayer. When the evening had come Jesus walks on the sea of Galilee to join his disciples in their boat. A thunderstorm caused the sea to be turbulent and the boat to sway vehemently.

When the disciples saw Jesus' walking towards them on the surface of the water, they feared that he was a ghost. When he shared "it is I Jesus be not afraid" [Matthew 14:28-31] Peter asked if he could walk on the water also. Jesus beckoned him to step out of the boat and Peter also began to walk on the water toward Jesus. Then something noteworthy occurred that we should all evaluate closely. Peter took his eyes off Jesus and perverted his focus with the blinding winds and the prevailing storm (i. e. circumstance) and he immediately began to sink into the waters. Peter would subsequently learn that focus is the Achilles Heel of Faith. By taking his eyes off Jesus he lost the ability to rise above circumstance. When the perspective of hope in God is contaminated by a misdirected focus we will always sink into the waters of despair.

Yes, you also can walk on water during a storm and rise above your situation despite circumstance and dilemma if you install and anchor a divine faith in God. One that is focused and stabilized on the will of God to empower, sustain, and deliver us through the storms of life. Peter's experience demonstrates how faith doesn't eliminate the storm but allows us to rise above dilemma. Habakkuk teaches us that a mature faith in God incorporates both His ability to preclude and/or sustain us when losses are eminent. Engaging the right perspective through the storms of life is a winning proposition for all who take hold thereof. Again, you also can walk on water if you keep your eyes on the Lord thru the storm.

Faith is not merely confidence but rather the right focus complemented by a resilient perspective. When God permits losses in a storm, He is also setting us up to demonstrate His restoration power. More importantly the agony of loss works a mighty work in the spirit like the fire which purifies gold. Peter said "Don't even think it strange concerning the fiery trail which is to try you as thou some strange thing is happening to you" 1 Peter 4:12. Something divinely curious is going on in our lives that we cannot easily ascertain in each storm we experience from cradle to graduation. One must embrace a confidence in the power of God that will serve as a fortress against panic and spiritual desolation to become a true Christian.

CHAPTER 7

Take Off Thy Shoes

Adversity often puts us on a path to have a one-on-one experience with the holy presence of God. You are not just a victim of circumstance experiencing random possibilities. Moses flees prosecution from Egypt after killing a man and finds himself starting what seems to be a new life for himself as a family man. Then he stumbles upon holy ground and finds his life about to be commissioned to serve the most-high God. In this chapter I will expound how adversity has a divine mission and calling. You are never a victim of circumstance suddenly imperiled void of divine mission. Academic theology cannot assert or promise that righteous behavior will preclude adversity. Neither should one assume that adversity is a punitive appropriation from God for disobedience. In fact, it is written in Psalm 34:19 "Many are the afflictions of the righteous..." which is curiously at best. This book is in a relentless quest for the definition, mission, and audacity of something called "good".

Let's carefully consider what it means to have a close walk or relationship with God. It's not really the product of spending more time reading the bible if you are starting to think a tad too theological. The Devil knows the bible, but that doesn't make him good. I trust you have read many biblical accounts and been edified by content; however, content literacy did not create a relationship with the author, or any character enumerated or referenced by the book. Relationship is personal, intimate, and binding by the sharing of interests. Consider for a moment what is required to develop a close relationship. Without hesitation it is easy to place sharing of values, goals, and objectives as the predicates for relationship between man and his God.

When we receive an assignment from God, he draws near to issue that divine mandate in the spirit. This divine "Near" experience may take place before, during or after adversity (e. g. the storm). A divine manifestation of the presence of God is rarely a response to a human solicitation. Neither is your divine calling optional or beyond your capability. The call and/or assignment of God is never corporate but rather a one-on-one experience. Finally, God never responds to a solicitation promulgated by the spirit of disbelief merely seeking to prove His existence. They that seek Him "must first believe that He is" Hebrews 11:6. His unsolicited still small voice is confirmed by his intimate knowledge of your prevailing circumstance. Yes, He already knows the details of your weary.

Your storms are necessarily prelude to a closer walk and greater revelation of Gods will for your life. Even then, your view and understanding of His divine plan for your life may be murky at best but be of good cheer. Your calling becomes increasingly clearer over time as you gracefully conform to His will. Your suffering is requisite to the presence of His glory and the manifestation of your divine call. The presence of God is necessarily objective. Following your God permitted adversity there will come a time when He manifests before you in a chosen setting, motif and/or circumstance with His undeniable presence and for some an audible voice. Recall the classic biblical story of Moses after his eviction from Egyptian Dynasty who stumbles across a bush engulfed with flames but void of consume by fire.

The Burning Bush was a supernatural phenomenon described by Exodus 3:1–4:17 that occurred on Mount Horeb. As Moses drew closer to investigate this phenomenon where the bush is burning, he notices it is not consumed, then he hears the audible Voice of God instruct him to remove his shoes because the place he is now standing is Holy ground. God calls us out of our comfort zone often through adversity to establish a new assignment in our lives for a greater mission. The place and circumstance that precedes the hearing of the audible voice of God is always Holy and reclusive. You cannot solicit this experience as a function of academic enquiry or in a congregational worship service to prove the existence of God. "They that seek Him must first believe that He is" Hebrews 11:6.

Please take a deep breath and brace yourself for what you are about to hear. A closer walk with God is not a promise that the sick, poor, disabled, broken hearted, or imperiled will be delivered as you have prescribed in prayer on their behalf. Neither does it mean the windows of heaven will open and all your debts will be paid with your barns filled with surplus. His permissive will for our lives often includes endurance of uncomfortable circumstances and unanswered prayers. His response is always fraught with divine objective far greater than what you have asked of Him.

Yes, some people you pray for may not recover as you hoped with all earnest and patience. Even after you have prayed in tongues, anointed them with oil, fasted, and wept a river of tears they're times when you hear radio silence from heaven. Be of good cheer! This simply means a greater work is being wrought in your spiritual life for a higher glory in the kingdom of God. Take off thy shoes … for the ground upon which you stand is Holy.

CHAPTER 8

The Challenge of Faith

Planet earth has been contaminated with a myriad of belief systems dating back to ancient civilizations. For thousands of years' man has sought a higher power to define his existence and to appropriate his needs for shelter, sustenance, protection, health, prosperity, victory, and acceptance into a divine reward when life reaches commencement. Each belief system has something man calls "God" residing at its highest echelon. Often an invisible authority with defined and/or assumed powers to suffice the said needs of his creation and/or domain of authorities (e.g., polytheism). You may learn more about this broad theological study of man and his God/s in a formal theological seminary. This brief expository is an essential precursor for the context of this book where we will necessarily focus on a common maxim between man and his God called "Faith".

The book of Hebrews 11:1 provides the classic definition of faith as "… the substance of things hoped for and the evidence the things not seen." Hebrews 11 further celebrates key progenitors of our faith as a reminder and inspiration for all believers in perilous times. Thousands of years have passed since the writing of that highly celebrated collection of accounts in the book of Hebrews. A closer observation of the accounts listed in the Hebrews 11 "Faith Hall of Fame" reveals a stunning similarity. Accordingly, faith is not defined as man's ability to trust God for the implementation of a specific prayer request but rather man's ability to comply with the undisclosed will of God. This theological precept cannot be overstated.

New Testament scriptures also seem to assert that one can pray for something specific and receive same by faith. Such a divine promise is articulated in Mathew 7:7-8 "Ask, and it shall be given you; seek, and ye shall find; Knock and it shall be opened unto you:" In a court of law this divine promise as written may be construed as a promise to appropriate a specified resolve for a given human dilemma as articulated in prayer. However, a well-informed prayer must incorporate a larger complex of divine events to be well informed. Romans 8:26 "...For we know not what to pray for as we ought, but the Spirit makes intercession for us...". When we don't get what we pray for something greater is at work far more glorious than the hope housed in our prayer closet.

A terminal diagnosis or a call announcing a loved one has suddenly passed away is perhaps at the top of life's list of storms that mandate faith and spiritual negotiation. Such cases will spiral the most devout believer into despair. All those miraculous healing scriptures you have quoted for years, and preachers have touted on Sunday morning now need a closer inspection. Not to mention the numerous miraculous biblical accounts that clearly displayed the power of God to do anything but fail. Now your Faith needs recalibration and a revised objective.

In fact, it really doesn't take a terminal diagnosis to challenge one's faith. Even an operable cancer diagnosis installs the doom and gloom of worst-case possibilities. What if it has metastasized to a different location in the body? What if it comes back after chemotherapy? Like any believer you begin mining for scriptures that promise resolve for the sick if one follows the prescribed protocol. Perhaps the most referenced healing scripture occurs when Jesus tells his followers in Mathew 18:19 "... if two of you shall agree on earth as touching anything that they shall ask, it shall be done for them of my Father which is in heaven".

The New King James Version of the Bible was produced in 1611 and uses the word healing 15 times, heal 46 times, heals five times, and healed 78 times. Healing is a major theme with diverse connotations in the Bible. Another classic verse often quoted in the bible in reference to healing is found in the book of Isaiah 53:5 "But he was wounded for our transgressions, he was bruised for our iniquities: the chastisement of our peace was upon him, and by his stripes we are healed." But is this a reference to the healing of our bodies? Many biblical scholars assert the Prophet Isaiah's reference to healing is not for physical ailment or malady but rather a propitiation for sin.

Nevertheless, what happens when you've exhausted all healing scriptures believing by faith, touching, and agreeing and your loved one dies? Surely, God has heard your fervent prayer and supplication for recovery. However, now your response to a terminal outcome has culminated a theological disappointment. You now have serious questions concerning the efficacy of prayer, faith, and the will of God. Nevertheless, theological disabuse will have to wait for now until you have adequate emotion to appropriate. Grief is perhaps the worst storm of the human experience. Despite the console of loved ones the agony of grief is left wanting. There is no medication or council that can remedy the pain appropriated by grief as tears beget more tears. However, the bible informs of a "Rod and Staff" filled with a divine commodity called "Comfort" in Psalm 23:4. I've used that Rod and Staff give me a minute!

Surely the biblical account of an all-wise God expounds resolve concerning our grief. They are found in diverse passages of scripture that are oft misunderstood or glossed over void of appraisal. Let's start by taking a closer look at the anatomy of grief. Grief is essentially bifurcated into a deep-rooted pain of loss and the agony of acceptance. There is no medication or therapy for the pain of loss, and no one returns from death. Hold that thought for now. You simply rely on time to mitigate the broken heart. But wait Not so fast! Maybe both components of grief have a biblical resolve.

Does God really know how it feels to receive a terminal diagnosis or to lose a loved one? The four (4) synoptic gospels including the book of Mathew, Mark, Luke, and John all share a familiar story of how God robed himself in humanity being born of a woman. He did so that we might experience His fellowship in the flesh as Emanuel which is interpreted (God with or among us) and to demonstrate his understanding of the human experience. He loved his mom, dad, siblings, and many dear and close friends to include one called Mary and her sister Martha and their little brother Lazarus and so many more recorded in both the gospel of John and Mathew. We all have family and friends that mean so much in our childhood years and beyond. However, within Jesus or Yeshua the Hebrew name, there is a divine dichotomy. He is both God and man.

The story is told in two (2) biblical accounts of a time when Lazarus a dear friend of Jesus had become very ill. His sisters Mary and Martha were well acquainted with the demonstrated powers of Jesus to restore the sick on numerous occasions from diverse ailments and conditions. This story is detailed in both John 11:1-44 and Mathew 26:75 where having watched their brother Lazarus's health condition rapidly decline, they decided to send an urgent message to Jesus that Lazarus's illness was grave and urgent. There was no 911 emergency medical assistance or emergency room to visit. So, they sent a friend on foot to find Jesus with a verbal inform that Lazarus was critically ill from some unknown condition. Their message was simply "please come as soon as possible our brother Lazarus is dying".

A living, walking prayer request was dispatched to find the whereabouts of Jesus our Lord. Excuse me. I need a minute to reflect. If you have never been taught this before or glossed over it in your bible studies, the spirit of prayer is a living institution that knows how to find God and deliver your cry. As the story continues, the prayer request carrier located Jesus and informed him of the urgency of the situation concerning Lazarus his friend and the need for Jesus to come as soon as possible. Please also be advised that prayer is not a vehicle of inform. Jesus already knew the condition of Lazarus before the prayer messenger arrived. So, it is when we all pray. God already knows the gravity of our conditions. Nevertheless, having received the message concerning the urgency of Lazarus's condition Jesus sends the messenger back to Mary and Martha with a confirmation that he will come.

What Jesus did not disclose to the messenger, was that he would not come immediately. Strange how we often impose an implied delivery schedule for God to accommodate our prayers without regard to a larger system of events that comprise the greater oversight of God. Nevertheless, the living, walking prayer messenger returns to the home of Mary and her sister Martha to inform them that he had located Jesus and delivered the urgent message concerning the rapidly declining health of their brother Lazarus. God has heard your prayer. In fact, God is the author of our prevailing conditions, and he holds an inventory of resolve for each human dilemma.

However, please be advised that on occasion God will delay or deny our prayer request for a greater display of His glory. Such was the case with Mary and her sister Martha as they waited for Jesus to arrive to keep their brother Lazarus from dying from his illness. As recorded in John 11:6 Jesus deliberately delayed his departure from his current location for two (2) additional days after notice not counting the time required for the journey. The story also shares that by the time Jesus arrived in Bethany the city of Mary and Martha's residence their brother Lazarus was not only dead but had been buried for 4 days as recorded John 11:17. Wait a minute! Can God Be Late? What if the bones were dry? Don't make me shout by myself.

The delayed arrival of Jesus to the aid of Lazarus was further witnessed by the presence of many friends who had come from Jerusalem to comfort the sisters concerning their deceased brother Lazarus. Some wept with Mary in their home, and some gathered outside with Martha all weeping and embracing.

When suddenly Martha received a verbal notice that Jesus was approaching, and she rushed to meet him. She was so glad to see him but her first response was "Lord if you had been here my brother Lazarus would not have died" [John 11:21]. Martha immediately sent a messenger to the house to tell Mary her sister that Jesus had arrived. This is a noteworthy moment to all readers who ponder where is God when you need Him. He's always on His Way. The Way of God is curious still.

When Mary receives word, that Jesus had arrived in the town of Bethany she and all those who had gathered to morn with her went out to see Him. When Jesus saw them weeping, he asked "where have you laid him" [John 11:34] and then He broke down and cried as recorded in John 11:36 "Jesus Wept". Wait a minute. Why did God cry knowing that He is well able to restore the dead back to perfect health and wellness? The best answer to this question is articulated in the book of Hebrews. So that we may know "that we have not a high priest that cannot be touched by the feelings of our infirmities but was in all manners tempted just as we are" [Hebrews 4:15]. It is consoling to know that God understands our sadness and knows the expression of our tears. He knows exactly how you feel when your heart is broken. God cried! ... give me a minute. God cried?

Both sisters were disappointed by the arrival time of Jesus which they considered far too late since their brother Lazarus had already died and been interred. Nevertheless, Jesus is now poised to display that he is not just a healer, but he is also the resurrection and the life for all that believe. And after he had prayed to the Father, he requested the stone of Lazarus tomb to be rolled away and called him to come forth [John 11:43-44] and Lazarus came forth walking in grave clothes and was loosed and resumed his life. God is never too late. No Never.

CHAPTER 9

A Plumb Line for My Faith

Life is necessarily filled with a myriad of measuring devices. Such devices serve as monitors to detect deviation from a specified law, safety standard and/or society norms. The speed odometer allows us to monitor our compliance with speed limits. The gas gauge allows us to remain aware of fuel consumption before we run out of gas. The weather channel informs us of environmental conditions before will travel. A scale can detect overweight conditions for health and wellness concerns. A physician can diagnose illness long before it becomes life threatening. However, how shall a man measure his right standing with God, lest He identify a plumb line for his faith.

The Construction industry is necessarily responsible for building safe and reliable facilities for residential housing, commercial facilities as well as buildings for a myriad of assignments to include cultural, social, and governmental needs. Such buildings must be constructed with suitability and safety as a priority for all tenants housed by such facilities. The building industry must ensure structural accuracy to ensure a safe, durable, and reliable architecture prior to end users/occupancy. All walls must be perfectly vertical, and all flooring and ceilings must be perfectly horizontal complemented by secure connectivity.

Each construction project uses specific tools calibrated to ensure construction integrity. Without such tools error will compound leading to a complete disaster for all tenants. Over the years many devices have evolved to measure the degree of horizontal perfection and the measure of precise verticality for construction projects. The degree of horizontal perfection can be measured using a tool called a level. The degree of vertical perfection or verticality in the construction space is measured by tool called a "plumb Line" which is the metaphoric target for the following theological discussion.

The plumb line is essentially a cord or string with a weight "plumb" affixed at its base. Because of the earths gravitational pull on the weight or plumb, the line is forced to align itself with the earths gravitational pull. This gravitational phenomenon creates a perfectly straight (e.g., horizontal) line perpendicular to the surface of the earth. The plumb line will expose any error in a vertical surface of a construction project. Comparatively, this raises a relative theological question. How do we measure our upright standing in the sight of God through adversity? Has God provided a plumb line as required for construction projects?

Let's continue our investigation of adversity and the need to install a precedent for same in the presence of God by making a few distinctions. The ten commandments appropriated by God on Mount Sinai and promulgated by Moses to his followers established a divine precedent for moral behavior in the sight of God. However, God did not promise that a devout adherence to the Mosaic law would preclude adversity. Allow me to reiterate, the mission of adversity is neither punitive nor developmental as many may assert. It is best to view adversity as an essential trial of our faith as referenced in 1 Peter 1:7 "…the trial of your faith being much more precious than gold that perishes, though it be tried by fire, might found unto praise, honor, and glory at the appearing of Jesus Christ". Perhaps the most important biblical aphorism to meditate as you experience adversity is that the trial of God is Holy.

It is no surprise that a biblical mandate for suffering of the righteous rarely receives inclusion and celebration in sermonic selections. Such messaging certainly would not draw masses, fill offering plates, or peek Christian faith. Most are seeking deliverance, healing, inspiration, salvation, console, and prosperity. Perhaps if we dig a little deeper in the sacred scriptures, we may develop a greater appreciation for the suffering of the righteous. We may also find the proverbial "plumb line" for which the integrity of our faith might be measured is gauged by adversity. Let's start with an intimate review of the story of a perfect and upright man documented in the sacred scriptures whose name is recorded as Job. The book of job can be found between the book of Esther and the frequently quoted Book of Psalms in the Old Testament.

The story of Job begins with an impeccable summary of his integrity, wealth, and piety. Job is identified as one "that feared God and eschewed evil" [Job 1:1-3] at all costs to maintain his right standing before God in all his ways. Pay close attention to this discourse. No fault was found in Job. According to biblical scholars, the Book of Job ranks among the oldest books in the Bible. How old is the story of Job? Well, if you were to fit it chronologically, it should be placed in the early discourse of the book of Genesis.

The Book of Job exemplifies a curious theodicy, concerning why God permits evil in the world, through the afflictions (A.K.A. Storms) sponsored by the adversary. The afflictions of Job as you are about to witness were necessarily egregious beyond any other losses recorded in the history of time. As we review the Job story, imaging yourself negotiating Jobs dilemma.

Job was happily married with seven (7) sons and three (3) daughters. His real estate included enough land to accommodate seven (7) thousand sheep, three (3) thousand camels, five (5) hundred yoke of oxen and five (5) hundred she asses. Jobs estate also included housing for all his support personnel and each of his children had their own homes on their father's estate not including the house Job shared with his devoted wife. In today's terms we would consider Job to have been at least a Billionaire. In contemporary church vernacular, you might say Job was "blessed and highly favored". But please try to contain any envy for now.

It's easy to want what other people have achieved or acquired in life not knowing the price that must be paid. Always remember, "For unto whomsoever much is given, of him shall be much required…" Luke 12:48. Nevertheless, as the story of Job continues the biblical account necessarily documents frequent sanctification ceremonies for his children using burnt offerings just in case, they had violated the will of God by ungodly behavior or intent. There was nothing more important to Job than to safeguard his family's integrity with the righteous mandates of God. If you have never read the story of Job fasten your seatbelts. This story is heart wrenching.

The story of Job commences with an extraordinary event where Sa'-tan visits the throne of God, which is recorded in Job 1:6 "Now there was a day when the sons of God came to present themselves before the Lord, and Sa'-tan came also among them." The impetus of such a meeting between God and His sons is undisclosed, but it seems Sa'-tan invited himself to what appears to be a routine gathering without him. It's not uncommon for even a man to meet with his sons when they seek his will and counsel for their lives. But Sa'-tan's presence provoked inquiry by God as the story proceeds. Job 1:7 "And the Lord said unto Sa'-tan, whence comest thou?". That reply may also be interpreted "Why are you here?".

God having all knowledge is never seeking inform, but rather yielding the opportunity for confession of intent. And Sa'-tan confesses that he has been seeking whom he may pervert against the will of God in all the earth. Then God asked are you now seeking permission to afflict my servant, Job? Job 1:8 "... Hast thou considered my servant Job, that there is none like him in the earth, a perfect and upright man ...". Sa'-tan then replies, "you have placed your hedge around him blocking me out and blessing him exceedingly well thus giving him reason to maintain his righteous integrity" Job 1:10. But "grant me permission to inflict adversity upon him and he will curse thee to thy face" Job 1:11.

Please brace yourself for the response of God to Sa-tan's request for permission to challenge the righteous integrity of Job. God grants Sa-tan permission to afflict Job with horrific adversity and establishes limits for the Sa'-tan to abide. Sa'-tans claim is that Jobs righteousness is only good when all is going well in his life. Could this claim of integrity by convenience also be true in our lives today? God responds to Sa-tan in Job 1:12 "And the Lord said unto Sa'-tan, Behold, all that he hath is in thy power; only upon himself put not forth thine hand." To paraphrase the response of God, he essentially says you may destroy Jobs family and annihilate his net worth but don't take the life of my servant Job. If you think for a moment your adversity is the punitive or developmental hand of God, keep reading.

Before we assess the personal and collateral damages inflicted upon this perfect and upright man called Job, let's establish a divine maxim. Got a minute? Can we talk? Contrary to contemporary theology, God is never victim of circumstance. He knows the end from the beginning and holds all power and authority in His hand. The afflictions of the righteous and/or unrighteous are all authorized by God with established limits for Sa'-tan to abide. When God permits affliction there is always a greater objective for His Glory. Although *prima facia* it appears terribly unfortunate for the recipient and their loved ones, always remember a greater work is in progress when one experiences adversity. How we navigate adversity is crucial. The profits of old convey useful advice when we are in the wheelhouse of adversity.

When experiencing adversity, Peter said "don't even think it strange" 1 Peter 4:12-13. Paul responds to the potential danger that awaited him in Jerusalem by saying in Acts 20:24 "… None of these things move me neither count I my life dear unto myself …". James the brother of Jesus says in James 1:2 "… count it all joy when ye fall into diverse temptation; ". Now let's Continue the Job story to see how he responds to the most egregious of circumstances ever recorded.

As recorded in Job 1:13 following Sa-tans unsolicited meeting with God and His Righteous Sons, he departs from the divine presence of God to wreak havoc on the life of Job. Please note that your adversity also has been approved by the divine Will of God with authorized limits imposed on same. Authorized adversity, fragile Hearts and tear ducts filled with crying each necessarily appropriated by the hand of God. You may not hear this promulgated in your weekly worship experience. Permit me to repeat, "Authorized Adversity" by God Himself. God is never victim of circumstance. In a court of law this evidence would be adequate to press charges against God for conspiracy to accomplish an undisclosed objective. God got a Way. Don't make me shout by myself! Give me a minute. Okay let's continue.

Sa'-tan commences his chaos with the theft of **All** of Jobs oxen and she asses by a band of thieves. They also killed **ALL** the servants assigned to care for Jobs oxen and she assess accept one. A calculated assault designed for only one survivor to convey the catastrophe to Job as recorded in Job 1:15 "… and I only am escaped alone to tell thee". Please recall Job had 500 yokes of oxen. That is 1000 individual oxen as a yoke is used to bind two oxen together in lock step. Recall also, he had 500 she asses and a work force suitable to provide management and oversight for this portion of his estate. The magnitude of this loss alone is enough to cause Job extreme depression and anxiety. But wait, this is only the beginning of a bad day.

While Job was yet receiving notice of the first catastrophe from a surviving employee Pursuant to Job 1:16 "… there came also a sole surviving shepherd, and said, the fire of God is fallen from heaven, and hath burned up the sheep, and the shepherds, and consumed them; and I only escaped alone to tell thee". Please recall Job had Seven (7) thousand sheep now all annihilated while he remains in grief over the loss of his oxen, she asses and managers of same. Please also note this servant's report alleges God as culprit of the assault on the herd of sheep. Funny how Sa'-tan can persuade human reason to issue indictment against God for chaos and/or catastrophe. Today most insurance policies necessarily include a clause entitled "Act of God" to accommodate losses that elude culpability.

The Story of jobs onslaught of afflictions continues as Job is receiving his second catastrophic announcement, he learns of yet another theft and assault. As recorded in Job 1:17 "…there came also another, and said, The Chaldeans made out three bands, and fell upon the Camels, and have carried them away, yea, and slain the servants with the edge of the sword; and I only am escaped alone to tell thee". Fasten your emotional seat belt we're just getting started with Jobs Day. Job had three thousand Camels which are now gone not counting the growing number of workforce casualties.

What we have covered so far should change your definition forever of what it means to have a "bad day". Brace yourself because this next announcement adds insult to injury and will surely break your heart. The Job dilemma continues in Job 1:18-19 "… there came also another, and said, thy sons and thy daughters … are dead; and I only am escaped alone to tell thee." Job and his wife lost all ten (10) of their children in one day among all the previous casualties. The loss of one (1) child is enough to spiral any loving parent into a deep depression but losing all your children at the same time is beyond measure of grief. The proverbial "plumb line" required to measure our personal standing thru adversity has earned his badge of honor. Job himself became the "Plumb Line" of faith for generations to come.

In all that Job had experienced in one day he was heartbroken but not wroth with God. It is recorded in Job 1:20 "Then Job arose, and rent his mantle, and shaved his head, and fell down upon the ground, and worshipped, ... the Lord gave and the Lord hath taken away; Blessed be the name of the Lord". Would this have been your response to such losses? Are we there yet in our relationship with God? Consider for a moment how you have responded to far less of a dilemma. Is your weekly worship experience feeding you the kind of Manna that inculcates a Job like trust in God, or is it just "... a sounding brass and a tinkling symbol" 1 Corinthians 13:1?

Phase one (1) of Jobs storm/adversity to prove the stamina of his godly integrity is now over. Sa'-tan has touched/destroyed all of Job's assets and family members with exception of his wife, yet his integrity remains unmarred. But wait, Sa'-tan's assault on Jobs faith is far from over as the story continues in Job 2:1 "Again there was a day when the sons of God came once again to present themselves before the Lord, and Sa'-tan came also among them...". Sa'-tans attendance of a second meeting with God and His sons once again provokes God's enquiry concerning his presence following his first violent assault on Job as recorded in Job 2:3 "... Hast thou considered my servant Job, that there is none like him in the earth, a perfect and upright man ...? and still he holdeth fast his integrity, although thou movest me against him, to destroy him without cause." Please note God takes full responsibility for the adversity of Job by appropriating a permit to Sa'-tan.

And Sa'-tan responds in Job 2:4-5 "... Skin for skin, yea, all that a man hath will he give for his life. But put forth thine hand now, and touch his bone and his flesh, and he will curse thee to thy face." Sa'-tan thereby requested authorization of God to allow him to assault Jobs personal wellbeing and health and he will surely breach his God-fearing reverence and righteous integrity. God then grants Sa'-tan limited authority concerning the health and wellness of His Servant Job in Job 2:6 "And the Lord said unto Sa'-tan, Behold, he is in thine hand; but save his life." Sa'-tan now has permission to inflict egregious illness upon Job, but he could not take the life of Job as he did with his livestock, servants, and beloved children.

Please note a common theme from the previously examined actions of Sa'-tan against the estate of Job, a perfect and upright man of God. In each case Sa'-tan had to receive permission and limits to abide by God for the affliction imposed on His creation. So it is for all readers of this book. Your afflictions have been pre-authorized by God with designated limits. Remember, God is never, ever a victim of circumstance concerning the storms of life. Now let's continue. Sa'-tan has just been granted permission to afflict the health and wellness of Job as iterated in Job 2:6. However he has not been authorized by God to take the life of Job.

As recorded in Job 2:7 "So went Sa'-tan forth from the presence of the Lord, and smote Job with sore boils from the sole of his foot unto his crown". Job is now covered with boils all over his body. Please keep in mind he is still grieving his prevailing losses in addition to what now appears both miserable and untimely. How Job negotiates his afflictions serves notice against the espousal of a victimization spirit, self-pity, or the punitive hand of God. The believer must install a steadfast focus on the continuous presence, love, power and permissive will of God. However, be prepared for those who are close to you to frustrate your integrity and faith in the Lord.

The record of Jobs physical affliction was further exacerbated by his wife's lack of godly console and encouragement. The wife of Job even questions the audacity of God to permit such afflictions on anyone as she offers her solution to her beloved husband in Job 2:9 "Dost thou still retain thine integrity? curse God and die". A more contemporary response to Mrs. Job insinuation to give up on God might be "Well, thanks a lot honey, I really needed that!". However, Jobs response is truly one to embrace as recorded in Job 2:10 "…. What? Shall we receive good at the hand of

God, and shall we not receive evil?". The integrity of Job remained untarnished through all he had suffered by the authorization of God. The grief an anxiety of Job cannot be measured and necessarily exceeds anything we have suffered by design.

Always remember, when trusting God does not appear to be fruitful there is always someone who will challenge the efficacy of your faith. If anyone suggest during your tribulation that "this trust in God thing isn't working" dig those heals of faith in a little deeper. And the Job story continues as his calamity is noised abroad like today's headline news telecasts. Today we might say, the news concerning jobs losses "went viral". The record accounts for three (3) of his best friends who came to visit him after they heard the horrific news concerning his losses. When they arrived, they saw from afar that Job did not even look like his former self, and they wept Job 2:11 "… they lifted up their voice and wept…".

Jobs friends also noted from afar that he had shaved his head, rent his mantle, sprinkled dirt upon his head and sat down in the dirt as a form of repentance for any wrongdoing before God. This curious ritual essentially serves metaphorically as a stripping away of all Pride of ownership, entitlement and/or achievement in the sight of God. Pride emits a foul odor before God and man. Even unto this day we often ponder if we have displeased God in any way when we experience adversity. Nevertheless, as the Hebrew custom mandated the three friends of Job responded in kind as recorded in Job 2:12 "… and they rent everyone their mantle, and sprinkled dust upon their heads toward heaven". It seems adversity may have been perceived as a recompense for sin in the Hebrew culture.

Now when the three (3) friends of job joined him and saw the magnitude of his grief, they also sat with him for seven (7) days and seven (7) nights and said nothing as recorded in Job 2:13. Job breaks his silence after seven (7) days of meditative anxiety. The prevailing thought of Jobs losses caused him to question why he was even born. In fact, the entire 3rd Chapter of Job serves as a tirade against the purpose of his existence. Job reasons within himself how it would have been better if he never survived his birth in Job 3:11 "Why died I not from the womb?" than to suffer such losses. His friends listened attentively in silence hoping in some way to console his grief with select words while inwardly attempting to contemplate the reason Job has found himself in such a dilemma. The affliction of the righteous remain curious even until this day.

Jobs integrity is pleading its case against a high court that seemingly has found him guilty of the thing he repented continuously as implied in Job 3:25 "For the thing which I greatly feared is come upon me, and that which I was afraid of is come unto me.". What do you do when the thing you prayed God would abstain takes place? Job is confident that his due diligence to maintain his integrity with God's righteous standards for living were consistent without fail. This is the point where performance-based theology falls flat on its face. Brace yourself, for you also are on a collision course with this resolve. To add insult to injury Jobs friends one by one contend he must have done something to breach the standards of God.

As revealed in the following assessment of Jobs calamity by thee (3) of his friends, it is not uncommon to have a default perspective of hardship as the punitive hand of God. Perhaps we all first consider our shortfalls to the glory of God as the culprit of adversity in our lives. The Job story is a much needed disabuse of punitive theology. This is a good time to remove the millstone (e.g., Heavy burden) about your neck concerning your prevailing dilemma. We all have sinned and continue to fall short of the glory of God, "…but in our weakness his strength is made perfect" 2 Corinthians 12:9. Nevertheless, this scriptural reference is not a pass for sin or an exemption from righteous due diligence, but rather a jubilant celebration of the Grace of God. "…It is not Gods will that any should perish…") 2 Peter 3:9. Without further deliberation, let's take a clinical look at what Jobs friends' thought to be the reason for his suffering.

Pursuant Job 4th Chapter verses 3 – 5 Jobs friend **Eliphaz** the Temanite mocked Job by saying in paraphrase "you have strengthened others but now you have found no strength or counsel for your own situation." In so doing Jobs friend Eliphaz charges him with both hypocrisy and inconsistency concerning his faith. Jobs friend Eliphaz also fails to empathize with the severity of Jobs losses and respective grief. Pursuant Leviticus 19:18 "Thou shalt love thy neighbor as thyself…", Eliphaz failed to consider himself in Jobs condition and how the last thing he himself would need is a contempt charge. This is a great place to press pause and contemplate if you also might be found guilty of same. The absence of compassion never bodes well in the eyes of God, who sees all things and knows the content of our hearts.

Pursuant Job 8th Chapter verses 6, 20 and 22 Jobs friend **Bildad** provides his assessment of Jobs hardships. Pursuant Job 8:6 Bildad asserts "if a man is pure and upright the response of God would be prosperity" and never calamity. Bildad further claims in Job 8:20 "... God would not cast away a perfect man...". This is to say Job should repent for all his wrong doings before God because God would never allow adversity in the life of an upright man. Hold that thought. The notion that adversity is exclusively punitive is void of biblical confirmation. We will answer the question of why God appropriates adversity later. Bildad also has the audacity to further expound in Job 8:22 "...the dwelling place of the wicked shall come to naught" further insinuating Jobs undisclosed breach of Godliness. Such statements were not only void of console but fraught with indictment. With a friend like this who needs an enemy.

Pursuant Job 11th Chapter Jobs third friend **Zophar** espouses a similar critic of Job as one who fails to recognize his own fault. Pursuant Job 11:2 "... should a man full of talk be justified?". Zophar further advances his insinuation of Jobs undisclosed evil doings against God in Job 11:11 "For he knoweth vain men: he seeth wickedness also ...". Zophar finally admonishes Job to repent and put away evil as recorded in Job 11:14 "If iniquity be in thine hand, put it far away, and let not wickedness dwell in thy tabernacles.". Zophar displays a curious insinuation that God would only permit this level of adversity if and only if a man has committed evil in the sight of God. Without question the three (3) friends of Job all share a punitive hypothesis concerning adversity which prevails even unto this day.

Despite all claims verbally filed against Jobs integrity by his 3 friends, Job maintains he has nothing to repent. Following the assessment of Jobs calamity (AKA Storm) by his critics he provides his assessment of their collective console in Job 16:2 "Then Job answered and said ... miserable comforters are ye all". Job further reprimands his friends by assuring them if they were in a similar condition, he would alleviate their pain and sorrow as recorded in Job 16:5 "But I would strengthen you with my mouth, and the moving of my lips should assuage your grief". As we continue the Job story, we find God himself was not pleased with the counsel of Jobs friends but permitted their collective assault concerning Jobs adversity.

Job responds to all by acknowledging that God is omnipotent, omniscient, and omnipresent with unmitigated authority to perform his will without approval or critique as implied in Job 23:14 "For he has performed the thing that is appointed for me...". Job sets a precedence for humanity to respond in-kind to adversity as he says in Job 13:15 "Though he slays me, yet will I trust in Him…". With such a proclamation, Job asserts "the storms of life" as part of Gods plan for us all as he also states in Job 14:1 "Man that is born of a woman is a few days and full of trouble". Perhaps, "ours is not to reason why" a quote from an 1854 poem by Alfred, Lord Tennyson (1809 -92).

The tree bares her apple, the vine gives her grape, the root makes her potato, the bee her honey, and the olive press her oil but what is the fruit of adversity? This question plagues us all as we seek to reason why we suffer, from cradle to grave. Something curiously relevant is being communicated to future readers by this record of severe adversity in the life of an upright man called Job. His consistent integrity and upright standing before God through egregious sufferings were impeccable. Allow me to reiterate, Jobs response to adversity has earned him the right to be called the "Plumb Line" of faith for generations to compare their own upright standing before God thru tribulation. So how did the Job Story end?

In the 42nd and final chapter of the book of Job God himself renders both verdict and resolve to the afflictions of Job. In all that Job had experienced and suffered not a single word Job had spoken was found to violate his righteous standing before God. This however was not the case with his so-called friends as each reasoned if anyone suffers such as Job did, they must be guilty of violating the standards of God in some way. However, the response of God was just the opposite as recorded in Job 42:7 "… the Lord said to Eliphaz the Temanite, my wrath is kindled against thee, and against thy two friends: for ye have not spoken the thing that is right, as my servant Job hath".

God further mandates a sin offering of repentance for each of the three friends of Job in Job 42:8 "Therefore take unto you now seven bullocks and seven rams and go to my servant Job and offer up a burnt offering; and my servant Job shall pray for you: for him will I accept: lest I deal with you after your folly. In that ye have not spoken of me the thing, which is right, like my servant Job." Please note that the repentance of sin also required the prayer of the offended for the offender to restore all collateral damages and personal losses. How often do we celebrate the prosecution and fail to pray for the offender? Following this curious mandate for repentance God restores all the losses of Job and extends his life for an additional 140 years.

After Job had prayed for his friends who mocked him, God removed all his afflictions and pursuant Job 42:10 "…gave Job twice as much as he had before". Job's restoration also culminated with a grand celebration with family and friends from near and far who prepared a great feast, and each attendee gave him gifts of money and of gold. The Lord also restored Jobs estate with twice his initial holdings Pursuant Job 42:12 as depicted in the following table:

Job's Former Estate Before His Adversity	Job's Latter Estate Following His Adversity
7 thousand Sheep	14 thousand Sheep
3 thousand Camels	6 thousand Camels
500 Yoke of Oxen	1 thousand Yoke of Oxen
500 She Asses	1 thousand She Assess

God also gave Job seven (7) more sons and three (3) more daughters. It is also recorded in Job 42:15 "…in all the land were no women found as fair as the daughters of Job". To conclude the calamity of Job God not only restores all he had loss and more, but He also receives an extended life span with health and strength pursuant Job 42:16 "After all was restored to Job, God extended his life a hundred and forty (140) more years, and he saw his sons, and his sons' sons, even four generations".

What does it mean when one suffers adversity without indictment? Shall the righteous suffer and the sinner go free? The Story of Job necessarily provides insight to this divine conundrum. Don't you dare think for a moment you can merit exemption from adversity by righteous living. The Story of Job predates the Laws of Moses which raises a specter of concern about how the righteousness of Job was informed. The Job story also predates the healing powers given to the prophets and disciples of Jesus in the New Testament. God is ultimately the source of installment for righteous standards for living and He is also the sovereign authority for which Satan must obtain authorization to afflict the creation of God.

The Job story is a clarion call for all believers to install a balanced view of the power and unfathomable will of God. The Job story also causes readers to question if their own experiences have been authorized by God for an undiscernible initiative. Perhaps the greatest part of the Job story is the itemized summary of his end state which far exceeded his losses. It is common to view God within the context of creation, provision, sustenance, and the prevention of adversity but we rarely consider His restorative power. In fact, grief is the anxiety associated with a permanent loss and the reason why a funeral is so sad. In the book of Ezekiel 37th Chapter verses (1 – 10) God provides a vivid vison to Ezekiel that demonstrated Gods ability to restore life to that which is dead both physically and/or in spirit. So ended the story of Job who sets the plumbline for right standing before God. Remember Job when going thru the proverbial "Storm".

CHAPTER 10

What is That Good? Roman 12:2

When God permits adversity in our lives the divine objective eludes intuition. All we feel is the anxiety, grief, misery, and misfortune totally void of reason. The prevailing question in the heart of the afflicted is why. When we seek to engage prayer and supplication to overturn the permit of affliction it is often to no avail. When adversity cannot be overruled by prayer, there must be a divine initiative underway. Something divine is necessarily in progress by the hand of the Almighty God. The bible is fraught with righteous men and women whose lives were decorated with horrific afflictions for which they endured for the grace of God. If something Good is working for us thru our adversity, we need to pause and take a closer look at the definition of Good. What on earth can be Good about a bad experience?

Let's investigate the notion and intent of something called "Good". Let's start in the book of Genesis of the Holy Bible. There we find the story of God's response to all he had created in Gen 1:31 "And God saw everything that he had made, and behold, it was very good". Let's consider this biblical account for a moment by use of inference. If the product is good, then the production was good. If the production was good, then the process was good. If the process was good, then the plan was good. If the plan was good, then the way was good. If the way is good, then the will is good. If the will is Gods, then God is good. Give me a minute. We may not be privy to the Will of God or His way, but surely, we can conclude his product is always good.

Now that we have established God as the sole source of good, we need to take a moment and examine the anatomy of that which is good. But first before we examine the anatomy of that which is called good, let's dispel the common vehicles used to gauge good. Good cannot be detected, assessed, measured, or quantified by human senses. Take a moment and think about what was just shared. This means you will not be able to measure good by physical experiences. That which taste good may not be beneficial for your health. That which feels good may not be in your best interest.

That which seems good may end up in a divorce court. Need I say more? Take a moment to reflect on all those experiences you have celebrated as good in your lifetime only to culminate disappointment. Now that the metaphoric kitchen is clean, maybe we can expose the recipe for a curious dish called "Good".

The word "good' has a panoply of references in the English language. Webster labored feverishly to be all inclusive concerning every variation for the use of the word "good". None of which could accommodate the Psalm 119:71 claim that "… it was good that I was afflicted". Nevertheless, for the sake of this theological exposition, "good" is the classification of any experience that has at least one or more beneficiaries. Please note the one having an experience that produced a good for another may have absolutely nothing to celebrate. Nevertheless, let's take a closer look at each of the two components of this hypothesis.

The adversarial experience always serves as the predicate for the good it yields however the predicate may be a horrible experience in and of itself. This is a curious dichotomy at best. Would God permit one to suffer for the sake of another. Yes … an egregious experience that you tried to pray away left you broken hearted with no trace of good. Something good happened on a Hill called Golgotha that was horrible for the one suffering but good for all His beneficiaries (e.g., Followers). Maybe your suffering was not designed to make you a better person but someone other is blessed by your sufferings. In such cases, one may question the efficacy of prayer as a solution to personal chaos and/or calamity without having knowledge of a greater glory. In the garden of gethsemane, Jesus himself was denied a prayer for the removal of "this cup" of adversity Luke 22:42 prior to his crucifixion. Gods answer was "NO" to his sons request for exemption from adversity.

Could something greater be underway that is not intuitively obvious in the predicate (AKA bad experience) in your life? Sometimes the hand of God is not revealed until we have the proverbial "big picture". Once again, the classic biblical celebration of adversity in Psalm 119:71 "It is good for me that I have been afflicted …" may require a broader inspection. This writer (Ezra, Nehemiah, or David) was only able to achieve this resolve by examining the larger context of their experiences. Maybe, just maybe if we take a closer inspection, we may find that adversity is Holy. Always yielding a greater good for the glory of God. Holy certainly was the culprit for each male, unblemished lamb who died for the atonement of another's sin having no sin charges of their own.

Let's take a clinical look at the beneficiary complex which qualifies the bad experience or predicate as good. Why did I say "complex"? Great question! The beneficiary is rarely singular. When the tide comes in all the ships in dock rise. The beneficiary of adversity even if same receives the console, hope, and counsel for endurance thru their own trials from loved ones. Additionally, the beneficiary of one's adversity may be anyone or everyone in their ecosystem and beyond. Yes, the exception to this rule is the rare cases where the one suffering is in fact the sole beneficiary. However, when the honeybee stings in defense of his nest, he dies a horrible death following the loss of his stinger. I suppose the honeybee thought it good (i.e., to serve a greater cause) to "bee" afflicted Psalm 119.

Contrary to popular belief, good is rarely expected to be the product of extreme hardship. That would be an arduous sermon to preach by any theological persuasion. However, everyone experiences a symphony of storms in life from cradle to grave. The proverbial storm includes every disappointment we experience including each loss. Finding the good in hardship requires a keen awareness and respect for the will and the way of God. Wait a minute! Isn't that exactly the mission of every pulpit message? Perhaps the most quoted scripture in the bible is found in John

3:16 "For God so loved the world that He gave His only begotten Son, that whosoever believeth in Him should not perish, but have everlasting life.". Let's carefully examine this scripture to see if it qualifies our hypothesis for the definition of "good".

God robed himself in the flesh as a son of man. He was born in a manger like an animal. He grew up in an impoverished isolated village. He Healed the sick and restores sight to the blind. He cleansed the lepers. He was treated like a heretic, incarcerated, and beaten like a thief. Then they nailed him to a Cross and pierced Him in his side. He Died a slow and painful death by crucifixion. They buried in a borrowed tomb. It is estimated that death by crucifixion could have taken between 6 – 9 hours of pure agony.

It would be a travesty to claim this experience as good until we take a detailed look at what transpired. In the proposed definition of good using the experience/beneficiary model, the crucifixion of Christ serves as the experience (AKA predicate). However, the suffering of Christ was far from good in and of itself. In fact, one would never wish such suffering on their worst enemy. Also recall, good can only be assessed for adversity if and only if at least one (1) beneficiary can be cited as a direct result of a given egregious experience.

To best understand the beneficiary of the death of Jesus the Christ by crucifixion let's consider the precedent. According to Hebrew culture specific animals were slain on the alter in the holy temple as an atonement for sin. Unfortunately, this atonement was a one-time solution for a specific breach in a right standing with God. Periodic sacrificial offerings were required for all subsequent breaches in righteous integrity and literally millions of male unblemished lambs were slain because only innocent blood could atone sin in the eyes of God. The beneficiary of each sacrificial offering was limited to the identified culprit or objective.

However, the agonizing death of Jesus the Messiah was an egregious experience (AKA predicate) that appropriated salvation for a continuum of beneficiaries. It is written in John 3:16 "For God so loved the world, that he gave his only begotten Son, that whosoever believeth in him should not perish, but have everlasting life." There is no end to the beneficiaries of the storm Jesus endured that appropriated eternal life for all who believed him to be Lord of Lords and King of Kings. There was no greater celebration of adversity than the Last Supper (e. g. Eucharist) that commemorates the Crucifixion of Christ. Thus, an egregious experience

(AKA Storm) can qualify as "good" if and only if a beneficiary defined by God can be ascertained.

CHAPTER 11

A True Story of Adversity

A certain man fell in love with the most beautiful woman he had ever laid eyes on. Her breathtaking beauty was complemented without equal by the sweetest of spirit. Her hair was filled with the most beautiful curly locks that never required the service of a beauty salon. She was truly a beauty to behold. However, just prior to seeking and opportune time to meet her, the young man was extremely disappointed to learn that the union between his mother and father culminated a separation after over 25 years of marriage. The young man, his older sister and baby sister had witnessed many heart wrenching arguments and reconciliations over the years until finally their parents decided separation would be best. The young man and his sisters loved their parents dearly but now had to choose with which parent they would reside.

Without hesitation the young man supported his mother's move to a nearby apartment complex and there he resided with his mom and baby sister. His older sister had already been accepted into a 4-year Nursing school program in upstate New York with campus housing. So, the young man became the support figure for both his mother and younger sister and occasionally visited his father to share father and son moments. His dad would always advise as fathers often do but such visits grew sparce as time went by. The young man loved his parents and was saddened to see what the family had become. There was clearly no sign of reconciliation as the first year past and very little communication if any between his mom and dad.

The young man obtained his first job as a computer technician at a NASA research center near Langley Air Force Base in Hampton Virginia. Life with mom and baby sis with no car for transportation was the norm. He borrowed his mother's car for all his social needs and was able to facilitate a ride to work and back home each day by the generosity of his coworkers. Until one day while glancing from his bedroom window he saw the most beautiful woman seemingly about his same age. She was carrying two large garbage bags to the nearby dumpster with another lady which he later learned was her sister in-law.

He continued to watch from his bedroom window observing her stunning beauty. He laughed when their attempt to toss the bags into the dumpster fell back to the ground. However, their second attempt was successful. She and the other lady then returned to their apartment which was right across the street from his apartment. Wow ... she's pretty he thought for the rest of the day. Little did this window observer know that the pretty lady across the street was also observing him from her bedroom window as he went to work and returned each day.

As time went on the young man realized an opportunity to meet a total stranger from across the street could be little to none, but fate afforded a curious opportunity. It was about 3 - 4 months of window admiration before the fall of the year set in. It was the time of year when summer was about to fully transition to the chill of fall. It was also the time when of year when the annual Halloween celebration took place. All the little children in the neighborhood would dress in exotic costumes at sunset on the 31st of October. They would then be escorted by their parents from door to door to solicit candy by shouting "Trick or Treat" at the door of each house in the neighborhood. The resident would open the front door and generously drop candy or fruit in each child's bag, and they would proceed with this ritual to the next house. The young man remembered how he did the same when he was a child and decided to visit the local grocery store before too late to stock a cache of candy for distribution from the front door of his apartment.

By the time the young man returned from the store with treats to distribute, the sun had set, and the "Trick or Treaters" had already begun to flood the streets of the neighborhood. The young man drove ever so slowly as parents and their children went door to door and crossed the street to harvest more goodies in their bags. Then suddenly the young man noticed the beautiful young lady he had admired from his window for months escorting a little boy in a costume from door to door. He thought, that's her, the gorgeous girl from across the street!

I must get her attention and say hello, he thought with urgency. So, he stopped the car, rolled down the car window and with great anticipation said, "Hello, I live across the street from you". Her stunning beauty almost made him speechless, but he gave his name and asked if he could call her sometimes as a friend. She said yes and gave him her phone number verbally as he peered through his car window. As he drove away slowly to his nearby apartment, he thought OMG! she is gorgeous.

Within a few days fraught with nervous anticipation, the young man made the first call and exchanged basic acquaintance information. Turns out she had recently divorced from an abusive marriage and relocated into the area to live with her older brother until she could secure a new career. After a few phone calls she invited the young man over for a face-to-face chat in the living room of her brother's apartment. The young man was ever so careful not to seem too forward and accepted the invitation.

In that first meeting (A.K.A.) date, they both sat in separate seats across from each other as they shared background details, personal goals, and aspirations. It was love at first site, which seemingly only happens in books and movies. Shortly thereafter came the first movie date, then the first dinner date, and before long walking thru the neighbor holding hands became a romantic dream come true. Like a match made in heaven, the love they shared became hard to hide. She was all he could think about each day, and he became same to her without conceal. After about 3-4 months of dating and visiting her in her brother's home, one night she asked the young man would you marry me, and he said yes. He also was fully prepared to ask for her hand in marriage the same night, but she was first to the megaphone.

Immediately following her proposal, the young man knelt on one knee and asked for her hand in marriage, and she also said yes. It was a night to remember forever. In twelve short months of dating the young man had gone from a window watching adorer to fiancé. Ironically, the young man's parents although still separated had begun to close their gap of separation with occasion calls and brief social interludes. Shortly thereafter the young man and his fiancé decided to secure an apartment where they could reside together as one.

They both secured inexpensive but reliable transportation and stable employment. Cohabitation would try and prove the relationship to be far more than a physical attraction but verification of functional compatibility. Indeed, with Oscar award winning performance they both became one institution before saying "I DO" they did. However, no date was yet set to marry. The young man thought there was plenty of time to negotiate a wedding date. Perhaps the young man displayed the typical male "foot dragging" tendency due to fear of change.

It was December 25, 1978, when early Christmas morning the young man thought it essential to visit his dad to wish him well and to formally introduce his fiancé as a near term daughter in-law. He arrived at his father's house around 11 AM or so to find that his mother was also there having spent the night of Christmas eve and the spirit of full reconciliation was in the air. They all embraced and shared joyous memories. The young man reflected on all the years his dad was Santa leaving all the toys for him and his siblings around the Christmas tree to behold before the sun peeked thru the dawn.

They laughed together and visited neighbors they had known for years. Then the young man invited both his mom and dad over for dinner on the first Christmas he and his fiancé were spending together. His mom agreed and his dad joyfully accepted and offered to prepare one of his sumptuous recipes for dinner. The young man and his fiancé left and said OKAY Mom and Dad see you when you arrive at eight for dinner. The young man could not be happier to now see his parents on the road to a marriage reconciliation and he himself about to marry the most beautiful girl he could ever imagine. What a wonderful Christmas this would be the young man thought with a smile and joyful anticipation for the dinner gathering.

It was a beautiful sunny Christmas day with an unseasonable warm temperature for that time of the year. A picture-perfect day to say the least. About midday 2 – 3pm-ish the young man called his dad to get an idea of what his father was preparing for dinner to see if he and his fiancé needed to prepare anything. His father assured all he needed was a kitchen table, silverware with Christmas music for all else would be ready to serve when he arrived. The young man's dad was an avid deer hunter who happened to have had a great catch for the season. His father shared by phone that he was preparing Venison Roast with wine sauce, candy sweet potatoes complemented with butter and brown sugar, macaroni with a mild cheddar cheese, cranberry sauce, and hot rolls. The dessert would be a good old fashion pound cake complemented by strawberries and whipped cream after dinner. The young man could hardly wait to sit with fiancé, mom and dad over a succulent Christmas dinner gathering.

The sun had fully set, and dinner time drew near. It's already 8:30 PM the young man said to his fiancé so they should have arrived by now. The anticipation of joy caused the young man to frequent the window to catch them parking so he could assist getting the food into the apartment. The young man also thought to fill the air with classic Christmas songs so when mom and dad arrived the atmosphere would be reminiscent of years gone by. After all what is Christmas without Nat King Coles classics "… tiny tots with their eyes all aglow will find it hard to sleep tonight… Thou it's been said many times many ways Merry Christmas to you.". Who could forget the classic "Winter wonder land with Sleigh bells ringing and people singing while joy is in the air" when suddenly the telephone rang. Somehow the ringing of the phone was void of the joy felt when Christmas bells are ringing. Then the young man answered the phone. Hello … Yes, it is … What! Oh, My Lord! The solemn voice on the phone said, "your parents were in an automobile accident, and you need to get to the hospital as soon as possible".

The young man shared the phone call notification with his fiancé and asked her to remain at the apartment in prayer while he went to the hospital to see how his parents were doing. Upon arrival at the hospital the young man walked swiftly to the emergency room and there he found his mother lying on a table but physically well. She looked at the young man, her son and broke down in tears as she shared "Your Father Is Gone!". He had been critically injured as result of the car accident. Then the emergency room doctor asked the young man if he would like to see his father and the young man replied yes.

A few steps away from his mom they had laid his father in a room on what appeared to be a flat table, where his blood-stained body lied still with no sign of life. It was a moment the young man would never forget. There was his dad who taught him to ride the bike and came home from work each day with a smile. The dad who had served as Santa for all his childhood toys now lifeless on a cold table. Christmas celebration would always be stained with grief for all the years to come the young man thought as he returned to his apartment to inform his fiancé.

Honey, there was a terrible accident and mom is okay, but my dad did not survive his injuries. Then the young man broke down in tears for a moment as his finance shared "it will be okay honey and we can make it through this together". For the first time the young man saw his fiancé was not only beautiful but now she is displaying herself as the Old Testament Prophet Nahum claimed of God in the book of Nahum 1:7 "… a stronghold in the day of trouble". She never left the young man's side through the wake, funeral, and interment of his father. Surely the young man conceded, this is the wife God has sent for me. In honor of his parents and to eclipse this tragedy with joy the young man set their wedding date for July 22, 1979, which was the same day and month his parents had wed. The joy of being married and raising a family filled the air throughout the 6 months of wedding preparations. The love they shared for each other could not be hidden from any that graced their presence.

When the wedding day arrived, it was like a dream come true that only happens in the movies. The church was filled with family members from far and near all to share the moment of union between the young man and his window found love. The spirit of love filled the sanctuary from pew to alter as they exchanged their wedding vows, rings, and the sealing kiss. The young man and his wife were so happy. Shortly after the wedding the young man was blessed with a great new job offer with a well-established engineering firm in Northern Virginia. Just what the young man needed to begin his family and career with his newfound bride. So, they packed their bags moved to Northern Virginia, secured a nice apartment, and joined the local church.

The young man loved his wife so much he came home each day at lunch time just to be with her for an hour in lieu of his co-workers. She was an avid reader of romance novels. She could sit for hours engaging the fantasy of romance. The young man new immediately that when she looked at him with a certain smile, she wanted him to go to the store to pick up an RC cola and a bag of Doritos Corn Chips which she enjoyed as she engaged her passion for romance. She was the apple of his eye and the love of his life beyond expression. His love for her was so great it could easily qualify as worship to the naked eye. Even the children new how much daddy loved mommy. The young man's wife name was Ella Mae Ewing, but her family called her "EL" as a nick name. Whatever El asked, the young man served with all his heart. Little did the young man know that the Hebrew names (i.e., references) of God all commenced with EL. The basic form El appears over 250 times in the Tanakh primarily in construct relation when describing the God of Israel.

Name	Meaning
EL Elyon	Lord Most High
El Ohim	The Great God
El Shaddai	God Almighty
El Olam	Everlasting God

Could it be the young man had fallen in love with a proxy of God? Nevertheless, the couple's vision was to have a large family with many children since the young man's newfound wife (El) had come from a warm loving family with 7 children including 5 boys and 2 girls. This vision was exactly what they both were on target to achieve until the pregnancy announcement of baby number 3 about 7 years into the marriage. With 1 daughter and 1 son, they both were open for either a girl or a boy to fill the empty highchair passed down from the siblings. They prepared a name for a girl and a name for a boy as most couples do. As the pregnancy approach maturity, the couple gathered logistics for the new baby including crib and cradle, toys, baby clothes and much more. Every member of the family displayed a joy of anticipation of the new bundle of joy soon to arrive.

It was around the 7-month of pregnancy when the young man's wife noticed a small protrusion in her abdominal area that seemed a tad strange. She shared it with her husband and the young man assured it was nothing to worry about honey perhaps the product of baby repositioning. The couple dismissed the concern of the subtle anomaly until the final prenatal care visit before delivery. In that visit the couple were excited the delivery date was near and the Dr. simply suggested to get the anomaly checked after the child was born. The young man's wife "El" said "surely after this child we will have more" and the young man smiled with joy. It was May 27th, 1986, when a bouncing baby boy was born to bring the total child count to 3 including 1 girl and now 2 boys. The couple was so happy until the doctor advised the young man's wife to get the strange mass remaining in her abdominal region checked as soon as possible.

The young man heeded the Doctors advice and scheduled an examination by specialist in abdominal disorders. After a brief evaluation, the specialists advised the young man and his wife that to thoroughly assess the abdominal mass a surgical investigation (i.e., biopsy) would be required. The young man scheduled the biopsy at the local hospital and consoled his wife with optimism that they would soon get through this ordeal and back to the joy of raising the growing family. When the day arrived for the biopsy, the young man took the day off work and after getting the kids off to school and securing a babysitter for the infant, he took his wife to the hospital for a thorough medical investigation of her condition. While the procedure was underway, he thought this is a great time to do the laundry at the local laundromat so it would be done when his wife came home. Immediately following the laundry dry cycle, the young man folded the close and stacked them neatly on the back seat of the car. He then went straight to the hospital to comfort his wife and obtain the good news of a soon to be recovery for his wife and family.

When the young man arrived at the hospital, he was directed to the room where his wife was still recovering from the anesthesia administered for the surgical investigation. He walked quietly into her room and positioned himself at her bed side since her eyes were closed as though she were resting and said "honey it's me, how are you? ". She slowly opened her eyes and smiled to see a familiar face. However, she had not been given a report of her diagnosis. The young man was assisting his wife with the inhaling unit required for patience to recover from the anesthesia when the Doctor who performed the surgical investigation walked into the room. His face was solemn, void of reception when he asked are you, her husband? The young man said yes, I am her husband and the Doctor asked would you come with me. The young man joined the doctor as he begun a long walk down a hospital hallway. There were no words offered by the Doctor concerning where the walk was leading or why.

The young man followed the doctor to an empty hospital room where the doctor had chosen to reveal the findings of a grim prognosis. The young man thought it strange that he had been ushered to an empty hospital room to receive this information. Then the Doctor said your wife has what is called a Leiomyosarcoma hosted on the outside wall of her stomach. It has spread into several of her major organs and appears inoperable. The doctor further shared that this type of cancer is very aggressive and is usually found in the muscle tissue of a leg or an arm. In such cases we simply amputate the arm or leg that contains the cancer. This type of cancer hosted on the outside wall of the stomach was extremely rare. Then the Doctor said your wife has about two (2) years to live.

The physician and the young man then returned down the same speechless hallway to the bed side of his beloved wife. Each step was replete with the rumination of the surgeon's death sentence. As they walked the young man pondered the biblical scripture "… is there no balm in Gilead is there no Physician There…) [Jeremiah 8:22]? How on earth will my wife and children receive this grim report the young man thought as he labored with acceptance for himself. Then the Doctor and the young man entered the hospital room of his wife who was then fully recovered from the anesthesia. As they arrayed themselves about her bedside their faces were stained with a hopeless expression that could not be concealed. The young man's wife immediately asked, "what's wrong?" and the doctor shared her cancer diagnosis and his commitment to do all he could for her. There by her side the young man stood with a face void of smile as he struggled to define hope and consolation. Don't worry honey, we'll get through this he assured his wife as she appropriated a smile at half-mast.

The bewildered couple returned home from the biopsy examination with instruction to continue treatment at the local hospital under the care of an oncology specialist. They gathered the children from babysitters and attempted to resume a state of normalcy at home. However, the young man could not get the death sentence off his mind. He needed to mask himself with confidence in front of the kids and wife while inwardly searching for an anchor for a proverbial ship rapidly taking on water. This is surely a time to draw closer to God the young man thought, as he pondered those frequently watched television miracles. In the interim the young man's wife resumed wearing maternity clothes to hide the abdominal mass that made her appear with child once again. Everyone in public places kept asking when is your baby due? Little did they know this child's name was "Terminal". Give me a minute.

The couple's first hope was to abide the Oncology Doctor's recommendation to obtain a chemotherapeutic resolve as a phase 1 attempt to arrest the rapidly growing cancer in the abdominal region of the young man's wife. Realizing time was not on their side, they immediately scheduled the chemotherapy while attempting to resume a normalcy at home for the family with a newborn son yet to be cradled in his mother's arms. Life was far from a normal resumption. The young man was now faced with the proverbial biblical question "Where is this God that heals the sick preached on Sundays and how does one get in touch with HIM?". The young man began a daily ritual of prayer early each morning before the kids were awakened. He would quietly step out of the back door to the outside pantry, bow his head and petitioned God for healing for his wife as the tears flowed down his cheeks.

Following his private prayer each day at the break of dawn, the young man dried his face so neither the children nor his ailing wife would see his tears. After all, daddy is supposed to be a rock and a stronghold in a time of chaos and uncertainty while inside his heart he was deeply troubled. Will God answer my prayer the young man thought each day. The young man also continued to ponder, is there something that need be done to curry the favor of God? Nevertheless, the chemotherapy was an abject failure as the young man heard nothing from God, the hearer of his prayer.

This aggressive cancer growth proved to be unstoppable by standard medical protocol. Then the local hospital transferred the medical case to the

National Institute of Health (NIH) where terminal patients went for special treatment protocols that benefited research studies with very little promise for the patient. After an adept medical NIH evaluation by the nation's best Medical Professionals, they decided to us radiation to disrupt the rapid growth of the malign tumor in the young man's wife. Unfortunately, the NIH radiation protocol would not only kill cancer tissue but all living tissue in its pathway. This aggressive radiation treatment was conducted at NIH accordingly and then the waiting and evaluations ensued. During this radiation treatment an attempted assignation of US President Ronald Reagan occurred and he was also rushed to NIH for treatment and recovery just two floors above the room of the young man's wife.

As the bad news mounted, the young man's faith in hope seemed to be under siege by each medical update. Days became weeks and weeks approached a year of daily petitioning God with tears streaming his cheeks only to receive radio silence from heaven. The burden of maintaining the family needs, children's hopes, job demands, and faith that God would deliver filled every second of each day. The young man fasted and prayed, sang in the choir, went to every church revival, watched every TV evangelical, read biblical accounts to procure a godly resolve all seemingly to no avail. Where is this God that saves and when will He deliver the young man thought 24/7?

About a year and a half into this medical saga the NIH Doctor informed the young man that his wife's Tumor had become necrotic, and the last hope was surgically removing the stomach and all organs damaged by the radiation treatment. The doctor also suggested it is best to call the family because his wife condition was running low on treatment options. Call the family? What are you really saying the young man thought with a void countenance on his face?

Isn't that what the doctor says when hope becomes hospice, and the end is near? What on earth do you want me to tell the family he thought day and night. It's hard enough to preserve the hope of my children with mine own faith on death-role the young man pondered. Where is the God that rained manna from heaven, healed the sick, raised the dead, brought water from a rock, quail from the sea, and defeated the enemies of his people? Despite a saga of daily prayers, the young man heard radio silence from heaven. Was Gods answer "No"?

So, the young man called the family of his wife to include mother, father, 5 brothers and 1 sister to come as soon as possible to share what may be final days. They all agreed to come to share in these trying moments of family despair. After the family arrived, they were all informed by the young man concerning the gravity of the condition of his wife. There was much love and hope against all odds. Family photos were taken, and they all laughed at memories of times gone by. However, faith and medical technology remained on trial with a compelling case against both. Give me a minute. Telling this story is far from easy to convey. Later I will tell you why. The medical professionals expounded the surgical goals to the family and groomed them all for a worst-case scenario. Yet they all held steadfast to a thread of Hope that had no promise of resolve.

When the day arrived for surgery the young man and his father-in-law sat side by side in a speechless waiting room during the 13-hour surgical procedure. As they waited, they knew any moment could be bad news for all. The waiting room conversation was void at best. The head surgeon kept them posted every 1 – 2 hours to confirm things were going at least as planned with no promises. After the 13-hour meticulous surgery was complete, the young man's wife was deemed stable in recovery. The surgical procedure was aggressive to say the least, removing her stomach, one kidney, part of her pancreas and a segment of her liver.

As result of surgery, the young man's wife would require intravenous feeding for the rest of her life. The young man and his father-in-law were also informed that the patient needed to remain in recovery/observation for at least 2 days before she would be able to receive visitors. The young man and his father-in-law both returned home to report the surgical results and to console the family with as much optimism as they could muster. If ever there was a time to pray, this was such a one.

After a reasonable night's rest and his daily morning prayer unto the lord, the young man gathered the family and shared the surgical results, scathing prognosis, and hopes for the days ahead. His window found love would now require intravenous feeding for the rest of her life. There would be no more children as envisioned. For some reason the term Faith now had a mandate for a new definition. Faith was no longer a vehicle of prevention or to resolve a chronic illness, it had become a life support system where all options of hope had been exhausted. When "If" becomes "when" God is calling higher. Sometimes God's answer to prayer is "No". Nevertheless, in such times as these God has a way of dispatching a divine candle that glimmers a ray of light beyond circumstance. God got a way!

After a couple of days with many hugs and kisses the young man bid the family of his ailing wife farewell as they each returned to their respective homes out of state. The young man assured he keep all family members apprised of progress or otherwise. In the still of the moment more frequently than could be shared the young man pondered why are we suffering? Where is the God that delivers? Dynamic preaching had become a sounding brass and a tinkling symbol with very little promise or celebration of deliverance. Church Deacons said, "He's Able" and Church Choirs sang "Heez Good", but none could promise a divine recovery. After recovery from the final surgical procedure the young man's wife returned home with hope to resume a modicum of normalcy. Having received such an aggressive abdominal surgery, the doctor forbade her to ever pick up her newborn son or to sleep in a flat position to preclude fluids from rising near her breathing channels.

A bedroom void of romance became decorated with bed pan, pain meds and medical logistics. The young man found his resting place on a nearby sofa in the adjacent room close enough to respond to every beckon and call of his ailing wife throughout the night. Despite a rigid financial budget, the young man hired a lady to reside with his with wife and newborn baby while the two older children were in elementary school, and he resumed his daily work schedule. One thing that became increasingly apparent was that God may not remove the storm, but He never failed to accommodate the needs of the young man and his family throughout the storm. However, the one enigma void of reason day after day was why this young church going family was suffering such an egregious hardship.

The young man never ceased his daily prayer ritual each morning before any of the family awakened. With tears streaming down his face, yet again he begged God "Please don't take my wife because I need her so". However, he heard nothing from heaven as he prayed this simple prayer each day for 2 years. He never let the family see his tears because daddy supposed to be a rock, strong in every way. Little did the family know that the little boy in daddies' heart was seeking God to embrace him like a parent and say "don't worry everything is going to be okay" from God. Nevertheless, the young man harnessed his faith, continued his bible studies, employment workload, and church fellowship throughout his family dilemma. Day after day, week after week and month after month there were no signs of improvement and no answer to prayer. It seemed God was never available to answer the phone or had other undisclosed plans of Glory in mind.

To add insult to injury about 18 months into the relentless suffering of the young man's wife, she contracts Shingles on her right leg. This new affliction was horrible to say the least and served as a mockery of a faith desperately hoping for hope. Shingles is essentially a resurgence of the childhood disease best known as chicken pocks. The major difference is the childhood itching sensation is replaced by an egregious attack on the nervous system which renders severe pain to the host. The last thing the young man's wife needed was another problem on top of a death sentence. Whenever a shingles attack occurred, the young man's beloved wife would collapse to the floor screaming in tears and had the kids go get daddy to help her back to bed in excruciating pain. Yet another item to add to a compounding inventory of misery while awaiting heavens divine rescue. The prevailing question in the heart and mind of the young man was why his family was under such an assault and when would God dispatch His deliverance.

The young man had not yet read enough scripture to hear the voice of Peter say in 1 Peter 4:12 "… Think it not strange concerning the fiery trial which is to try you...". Neither had the young studied enough scripture to hear the response of Paul when he became aware of the eminent threats against his very life in Acts 20:24 "But none of these things move me, neither count I my life dear unto myself, so that I might finish my course with joy...". The young man had yet still to acquaint himself with Job 13:15 "... though He slay me yet will I trust in Him..." after Job lost all 10 of his children and all his wealth in one day. Maybe misery could use the right company in those weakest hours. Yet still, the young man pressed onward to secure a hope against hope day after day despite despair.

As time progressed the young man's wife was able to manage the pain associated with shingles with a prescription of morphine prescribed by her doctor. However, she progressively lost weight due to the absence of solid foods in her diet surviving solely on an intravenous nutrition. Her voluptuous beauty displayed on their wedding day had dwindled to an 84-pound skeletal structure. Still no answer to prayer of blessed assurance as promulgated from the preachers' lectern and no sign of improvement to credit to medical protocol. The only thing unscathed was their relentless love for each other. She was only 31 and he 32 years young. This was not supposed to be happening to anyone at this age with 3 babies to raise. And then there came a day the young man and his wife experienced a Romeo and Juliet moment while the children were in bed and just the two of them were together in the room ruminating the severity of the situation.

The moment that was shared between the young couple is best describes as the classic Shakespearean story of *Romeo and Juliet* belonging to a tradition of tragic <u>romances</u> stretching back to 1562. Romeo and Juliet fell so deeply in love that one could not live without the other. In the Shakespearean play Romeo finds Juliet in a drug induced sleep, he poisoned himself to death to be with her eternally thinking she was dead. When Juliet awakened and found Romeo deceased, she stabs herself with his dagger and joins him in death. Just as Romeo and Juliet contemplated life without the other as not worth living, the young man said to his wife if you die, I will also take my life to be with you still. It was the most profound expression of love the young man had ever uttered to anyone with a sincere commitment void of even the flinch of an eye.

When his dying wife saw in his eyes that his love for her was without measure, her maternal instinct immediately thought of the children without any parents and the pain they would bear. Her response to the young man was "No you must raise the kids if anything should happen to me". The young man's reply to his ailing wife was a stint of silence for he loved the children also. His agreement to be the surviving parent was conceded with a paralytic tongue stricken with silence. Nevertheless, the depth of their expression of a sincere love for each other will live forever. As time went on, the young man's wife became more bed stricken and the young man drew closer to God through daily bible studies and fasting. The local church invited him to support a Thursday night bible study and the young man accepted the offer hoping it would curry favor with the God who is able to do anything but fail.

The more time past the more the young man emerged himself in the wake of Gods glory, often referenced by many as the word of God. It somehow offered an eclipse to the waning hope of deliverance but had no resolve to the declining health of his beloved wife. She also emerged herself in daily devotions for biblical consolation in the words of the prophet Isaiah 53:5 who said, "But he was wounded for our transgressions, he was bruised for our iniquities: the chastisement of our peace was upon him; and by his stripes we are healed." As the end drew near the young man's wife quoted this scripture from sunup to sundown seeking comfort from the words of Isaiah. And a night came when the young man was studying the bible at the kitchen table when he heard a strange mummering sound from his wife seemingly asleep in bed.

He rushed into the bedroom to find his wife murmuring "I am alive, I am alive, I am alive" repeatedly but her lips were barely moving. The young man embraced her, and she seemed to stabilize. Not knowing how to interpret the incident or the urgency thereof the young man called an ambulance and proceeded to disconnect her IV so she would be prepared to be transported to a hospital to obtain a medical evaluation. It was there in the bedroom he had his last conversation with his wife. She gazed as it were at the ceiling of the room and heaven only knows what she saw but then she turned to her husband and said, "you will have to raise the kids". The young man promptly responding, "No we will raise them together" we'll make it thru this together. Within minutes the ambulance arrived and entered the house. The young man's wife had gotten back in bed and seemed stable and back to herself when the medical techs entered the bedroom.

All seemed well for the first few minutes as the bedside medics asked a few questions concerning the symptoms of the young man's wife, when suddenly her eyes rolled back, and she slipped into an unconscious state. The medics rushed to get the stretcher from the ambulance into the house and transferred the young man's wife from her bed to the stretcher. After several attempts to revive her in the bedroom with no response using the electro-cardio shocking device she was rushed by ambulance to the hospital. The young man got all the kids to a nearby neighbor and made his way alone to the hospital as fast as he could. No time to pray or petition God for resolve. Thoughts of survival and recovery for his wife dominated the young man's thoughts.

When the young man arrived at the emergency room of the Hospital, he was ushered to a small waiting room where he sat alone hoping for the best. The medics were desperately working to revive his wife from a non-responsive state. There were no words to describe the fear and anxiety that filled the waiting room as the young man waited for an update on his wife's condition. The wait was fraught with a timeless hope and a state of mental paralysis. When suddenly the Doctor walked into the waiting room and shared that the young man's wife was non-responsive still as he requested permission for a last resort procedure. When the medic saw the young man was speechless, he lowered his head and said, "I guess you want us to do all we can" and returned to the emergency room.

After about 15 - 20 minutes later, the same Doctor who had announced permission to conduct his final recovery attempt returned with the worst news the young man could hear. The young man looked as the Doctor entered the room and saw the look of regret on his face as he announced, "We did all we could". This the young man decoded to mean one thing only as he stood slowly to his feet and pondered my wife, my love, the mother of my children is gone. When the Doctor asked if the young man wanted to see his wife, no words could find a resting place in his tongue. He simply nodded his reply and followed the doctor down a short corridor to a small room where she laid. Before the young man could enter room, he saw his window found love laying lifeless on a table and her skin appeared almost purple as if she had suffocated in her final moments.

The sight of his wife's motionless body and her appearance was unbearable as the young man paused then turned away never entering the room for a bedside view. The Doctor ushered him back to the waiting room still speechless from the image of his lifeless love. After a few moments the doctor returned with a brown paper bag filled with the personal belongings of the young man's wife for him to carry home. As the Doctor handed him the bag, he also offered to facilitate a ride home and the young man's response was a speechless nod that implied "No thanks I can make it home". Inside the brown paper bag was his blood-stained shirt which his wife had used for a night gown, the watch which he gave her for her birthday and the diamond ring and wedding band he slipped on her finger that consummated their bond in marriage.

The young man returned home to gather his children and trusted God for a family healing from such a tragedy and loss over time. Excuse me ... I need a tissue. Seems like just yesterday. By now you may have pondered who is the young man in this story? Well, the young man in this story is in fact the author of this book and those three little children that called me daddy as toddlers are now adults with established professional careers with children of their own. However, the stain of this memory lives on and gives us all hope of reunion in heaven. Yes, sometimes God says No to some of our prayers, but be of good cheer. He will never leave us nor forsake us.

Just as we all ponder why we suffer and why some prayers seem to be stayed by the Hand of God, be of good courage. A mighty work beyond our ability to gauge and comprehend is underway by His divine power. The Faith and suffering of my wife pushed me closer to God and now many shall benefit from the stain of our story. Truly one who suffers by the grace of God shall not only be blessed eternally, but they shall also empower and anoint a host of beneficiaries. Authorized Adversity is Holy!

I must go for now, but always remember "God doesn't make a way, He is the way!"

"For I reckon that the sufferings of this present time are not worthy to be compared with the Glory which shall be revealed in us" Romans 8:18

"Many are the afflictions of the righteous, but God delivers us from them all" Psalm 34:19

Now ... "take up your cross and follow me" Mathew 6:24

"It was good that I was afflicted" Psalm 119:71
A Celebration of Adversity

www.ingramcontent.com/pod-product-compliance
Lightning Source LLC
LaVergne TN
LVHW020441070526
838199LV00063B/4807